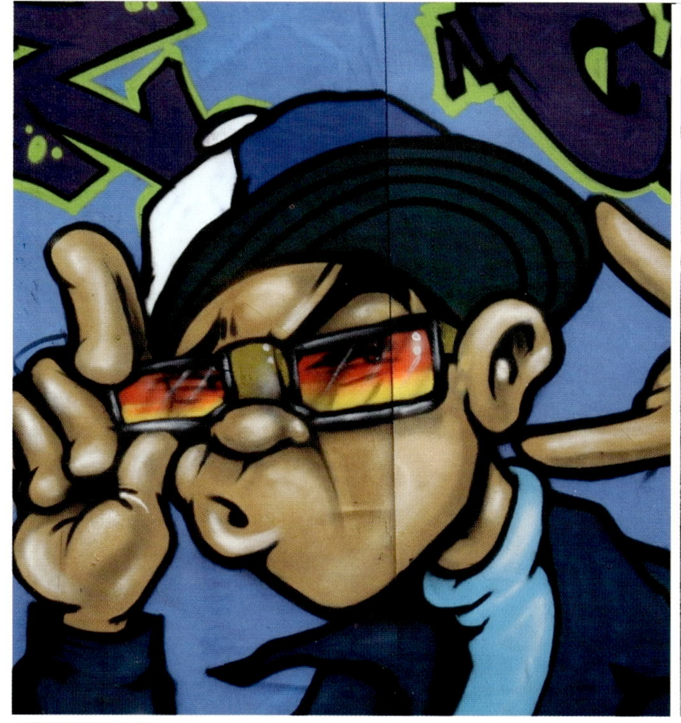
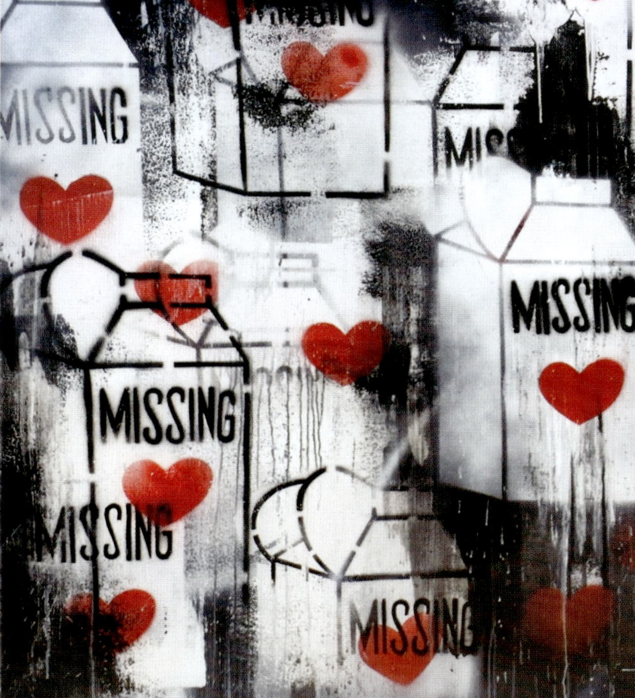

ON THE WALL POSTERS:

STREET ART

30 Graffiti-Inspired Wall Posters to TEAR OUT and HANG UP

SUPERFLAT NB

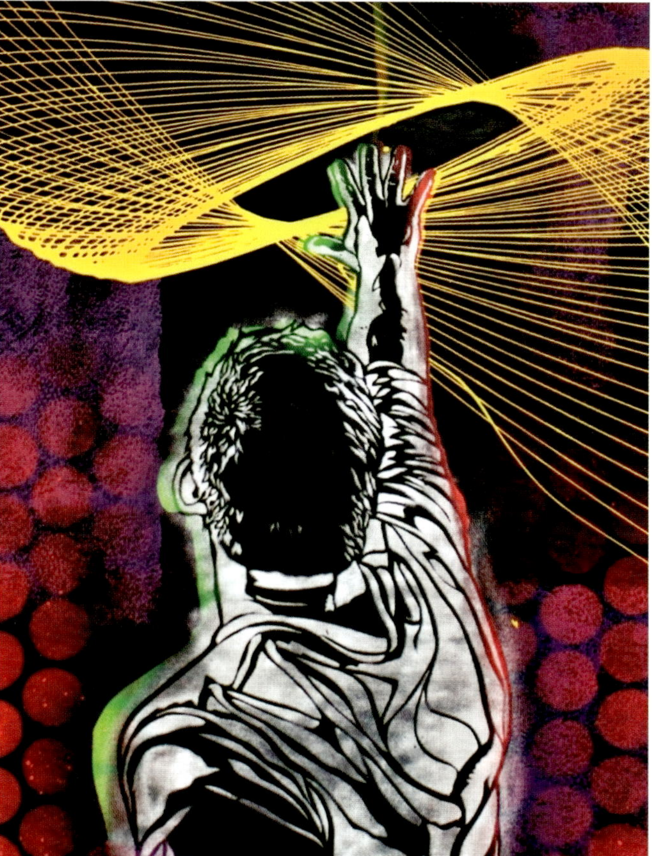
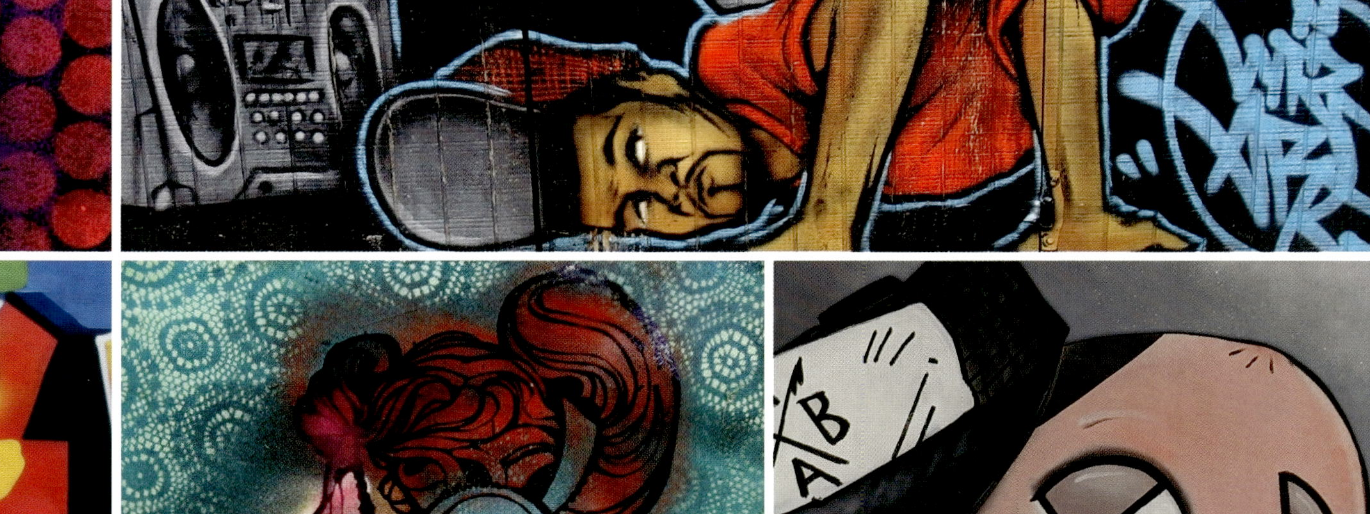
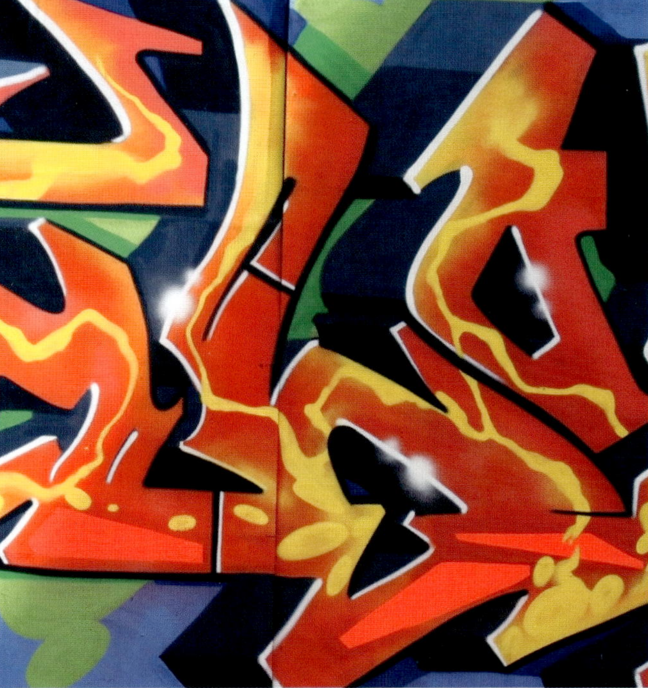
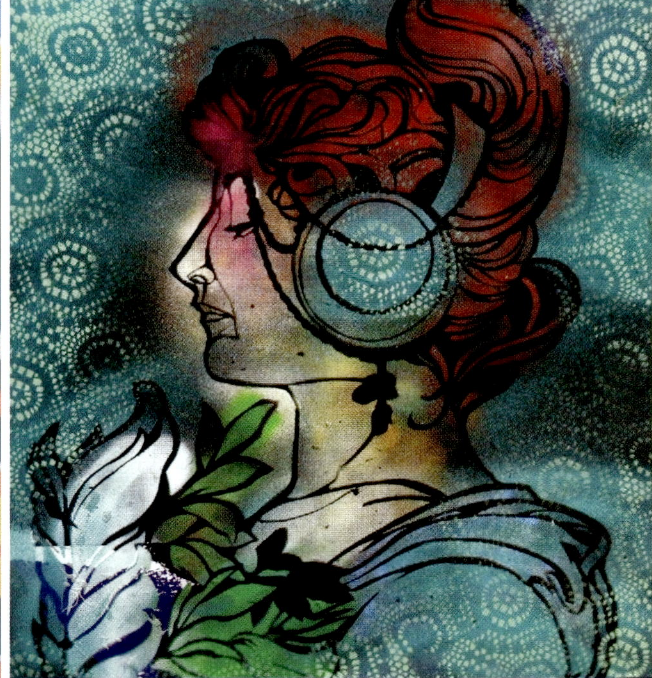
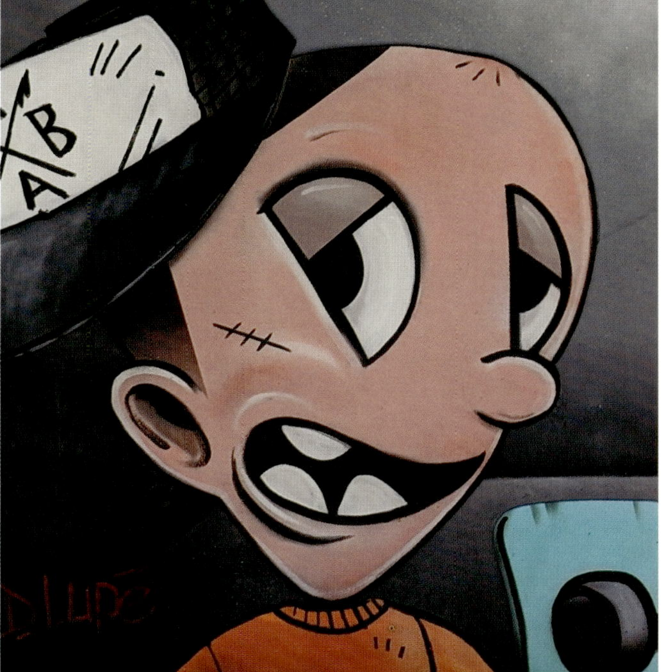

ADAMS MEDIA

NEW YORK   LONDON   TORONTO   SYDNEY   NEW DELHI

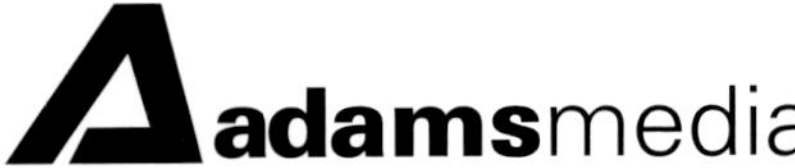

Adams Media
An Imprint of Simon & Schuster, Inc.
100 Technology Center Drive
Stoughton, Massachusetts 02072

First Adams Media trade paperback edition September 2023

ADAMS MEDIA and colophon are registered trademarks of Simon & Schuster, Inc.

For information about special discounts for bulk purchases, please contact Simon & Schuster Special Sales at 1-866-506-1949 or business@simonandschuster.com.

The Simon & Schuster Speakers Bureau can bring authors to your live event. For more information or to book an event, contact the Simon & Schuster Speakers Bureau at 1-866-248-3049 or visit our website at www.simonspeakers.com.

Interior design by Erin Alexander

Manufactured in China

10   9   8   7   6   5   4   3   2   1

ISBN 978-1-5072-2099-3

INTRODUCTION

The evolution of art in the streets has shaped the way many of us see the world. It has quickly become a way for people to express themselves and create their own voice. Today, street art is used worldwide for self-expression and to add character to unexpected places. Experience the art around you by bringing this collection of thirty expressive prints in *On the Wall Posters: Street Art* into your own space.

From wildstyle graffiti tags and colorful B-boy characters to pop art, stencil-style murals, and more, these posters transform any room. A collection by friends of Superflat NB—a group that facilitates public art throughout New Bedford, Massachusetts, while providing more access to the arts—these prints are the perfect way to personalize and customize an area, whether you are decorating your bedroom, dorm room, apartment, or other living space. Each poster is 11" × 14" and comes with perforated edges for easy removal. Choose your favorites, tear them out, and give your eyes something interesting to look at.

These posters work well either alone or as a group for a dynamic poster wall. Hang one as a colorful focal point or hang multiple in a grid, cool shape, or however else you decide for a high-impact wall. No matter how you use them, these mural prints are sure to create a bold space that you'll actually want to hang out in.

Use your walls to make a statement with *On the Wall Posters: Street Art*.

ABOUT SUPERFLAT NB

Superflat NB is lowering the barriers to the access of art in New Bedford, Massachusetts. Founded in 2017, the group is dedicated to beautifying its hometown by giving local, national, and international artists a role in creating art throughout the city of New Bedford. Its aim is to foster pride and ownership of shared spaces through public art while supporting inclusive environments where anybody can experience great art.

Takashi Murakami coined the term "Superflat" to express spatial compression and the blending of high and low art in his own work. Inspired by Murakami, Superflat NB provides access to the arts by directly engaging New Bedford's youth, artists, and residents in the ideation and creation of transformative public art through the traditions of mural making.

Superflat NB leverages the good work of other organizations in the community, such as 3rd EyE Unlimited; New Bedford Creative; mediumstudio; the Co-Creative Center; DBM; BigB; MassDevelopment; Massachusetts Design, Art, and Technology Institute (DATMA); the Barr Foundation; state and local government; New Bedford Public Schools; New Bedford Housing Authority; the SouthCoast Community Foundation; and New Bedford Art Museum/Artworks! Serving young people is central to its efforts. Superflat NB wants to inspire younger generations—and be inspired by them. Through its programming and partnerships, Superflat NB helps people explore culture in new ways—and expand their social networks and connections to resources and opportunities. Learn more at SuperflatNB.org.

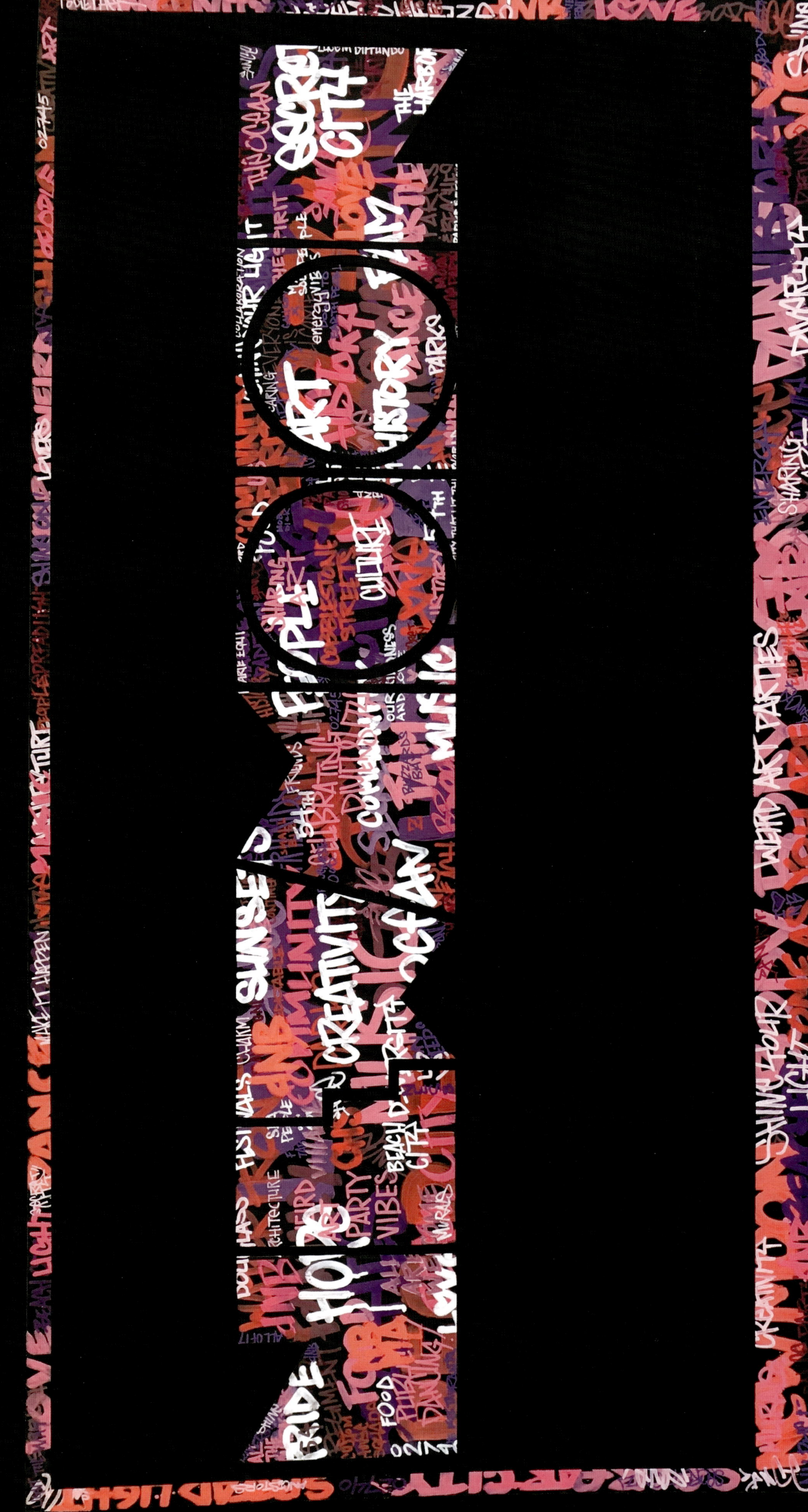

New Moon

Artist: Mandy Fraser
Commissioned by: New Moon
Location: Co-Creative Center, New Bedford, Massachusetts
Photographer: Mandy Fraser

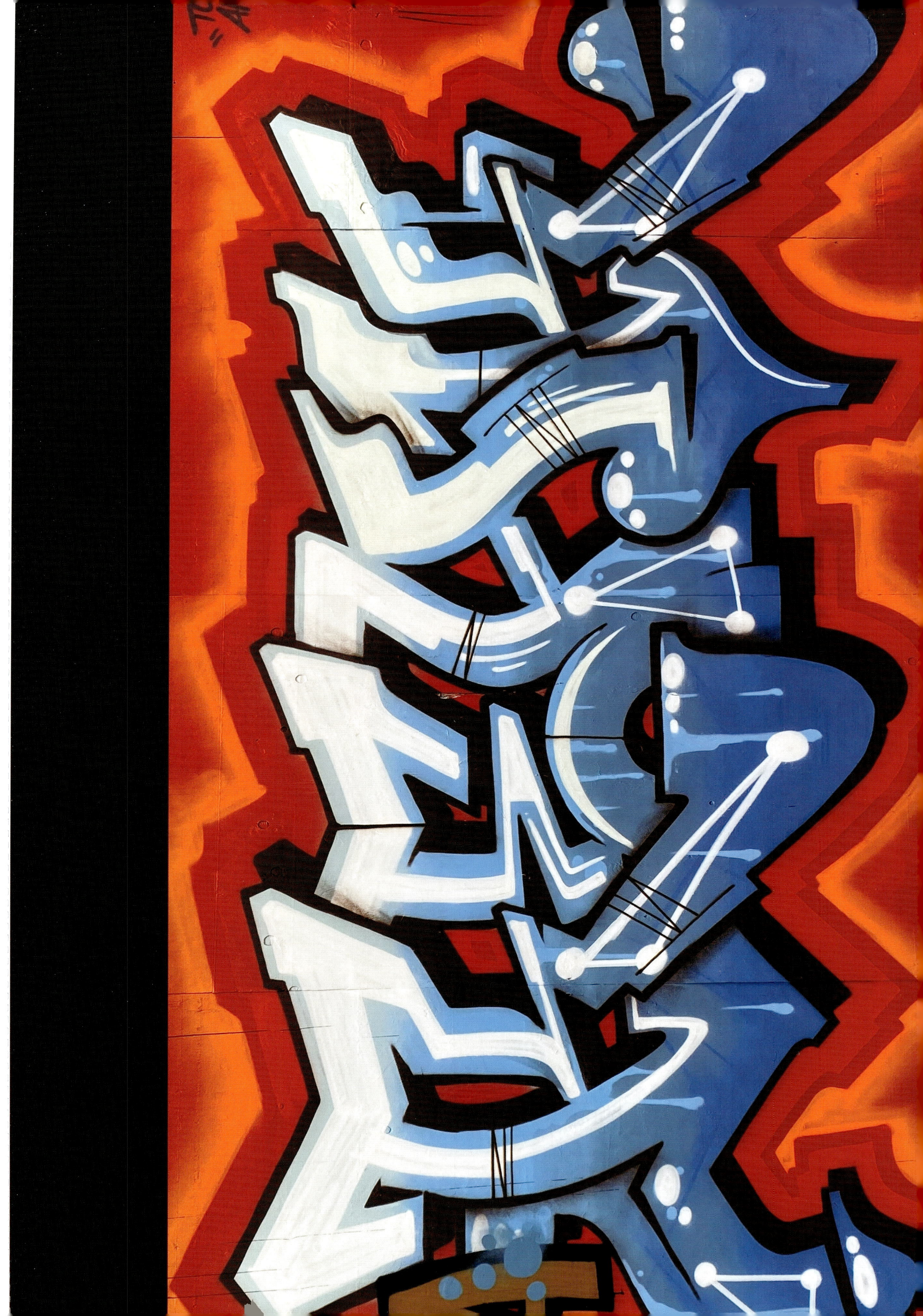

REAK

Artist: REAK VA Outcasts
Commissioned by: 3rd EyE Open
Location: Wing's Court, New Bedford, Massachusetts
Photographer: Kim Goddard

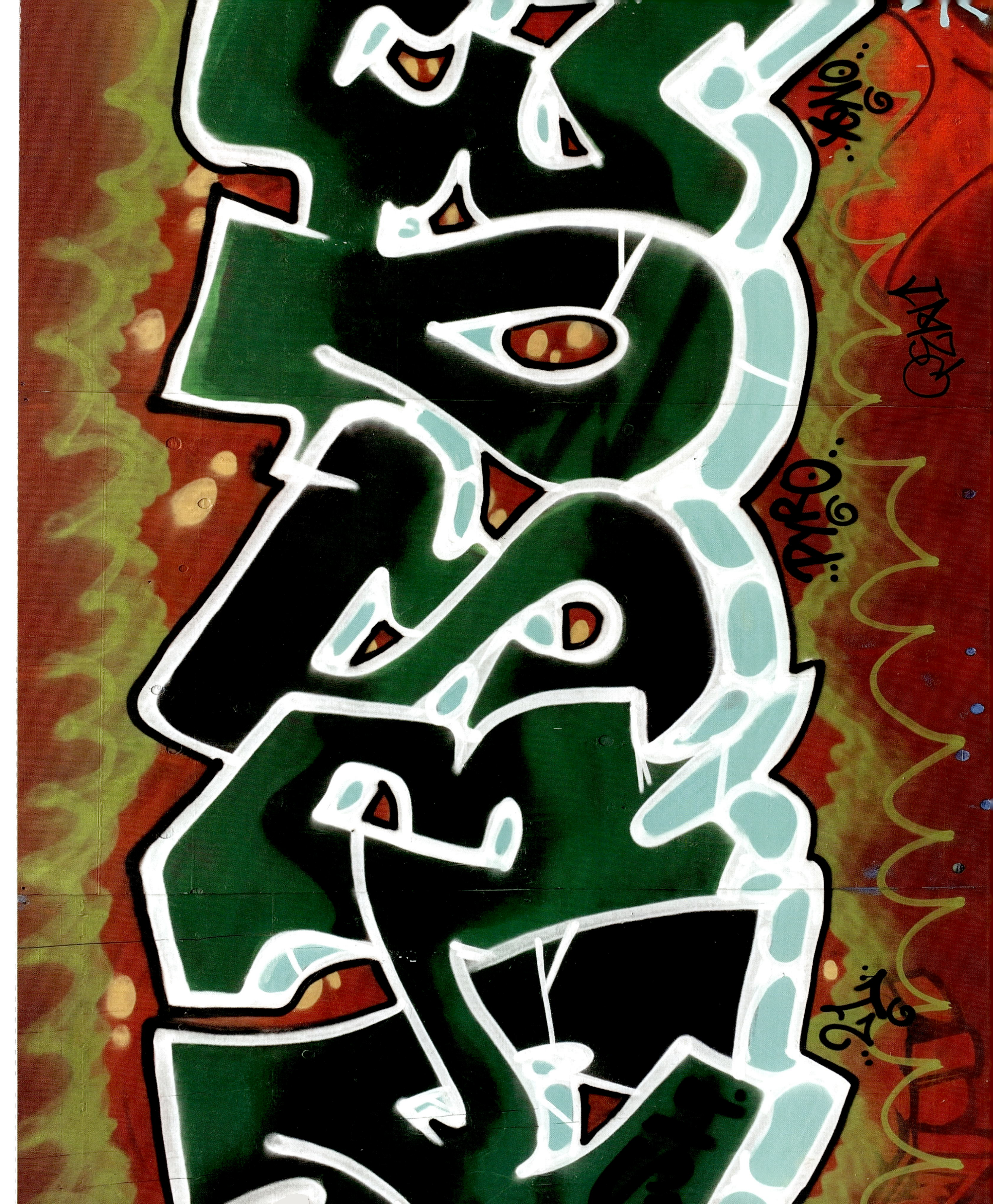

ABSOE

Artist: ABSOE
Commissioned by: 3rd EyE Open
Location: Wing's Court, New Bedford, Massachusetts
Photographer: Kim Goddard

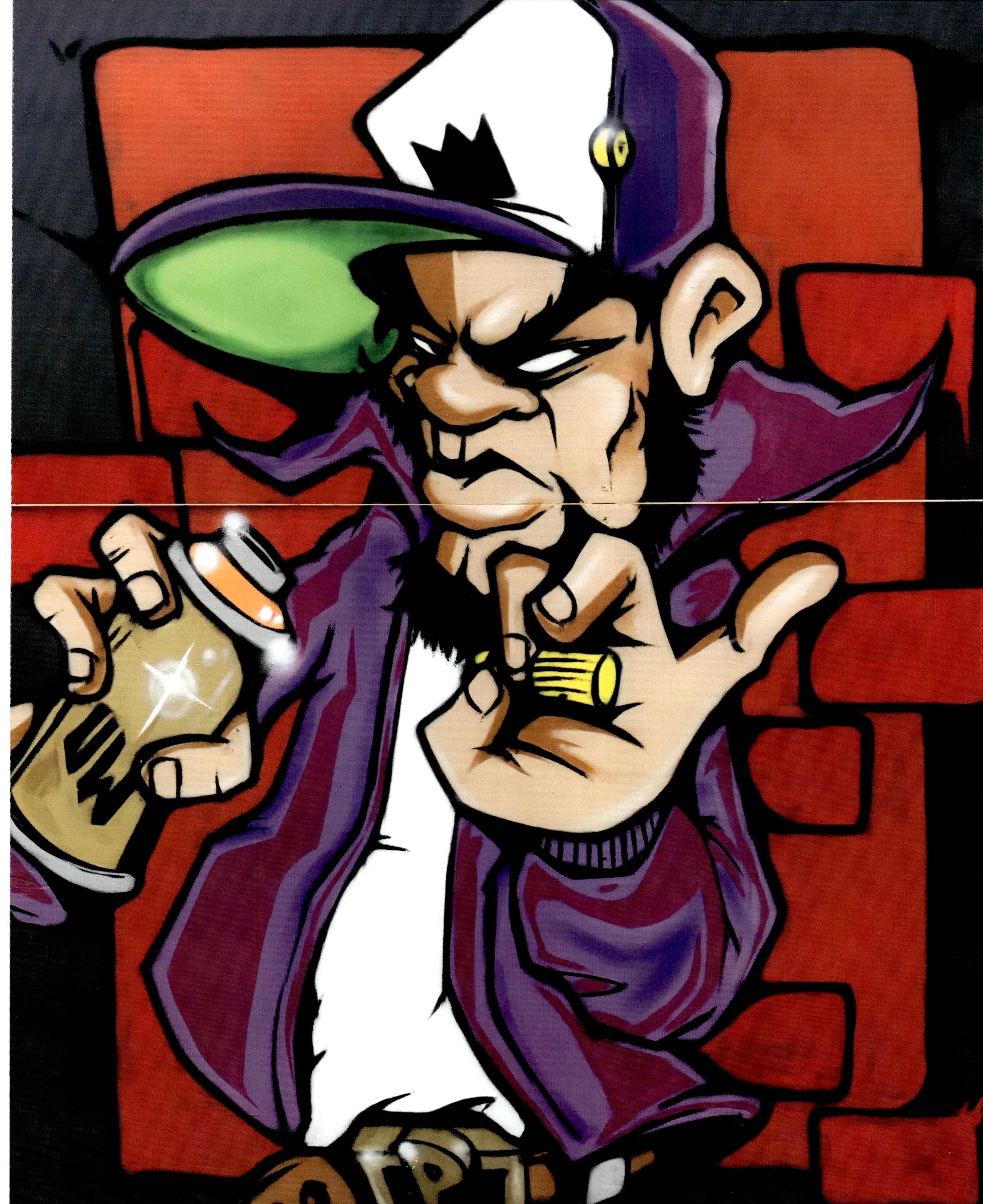

PFunk BBoy

Artist: PFunk UW DOA
Commissioned by: 3rd EyE Open
Location: New Bedford Whaling National Historical Park, New Bedford, Massachusetts
Photographer: Kim Goddard

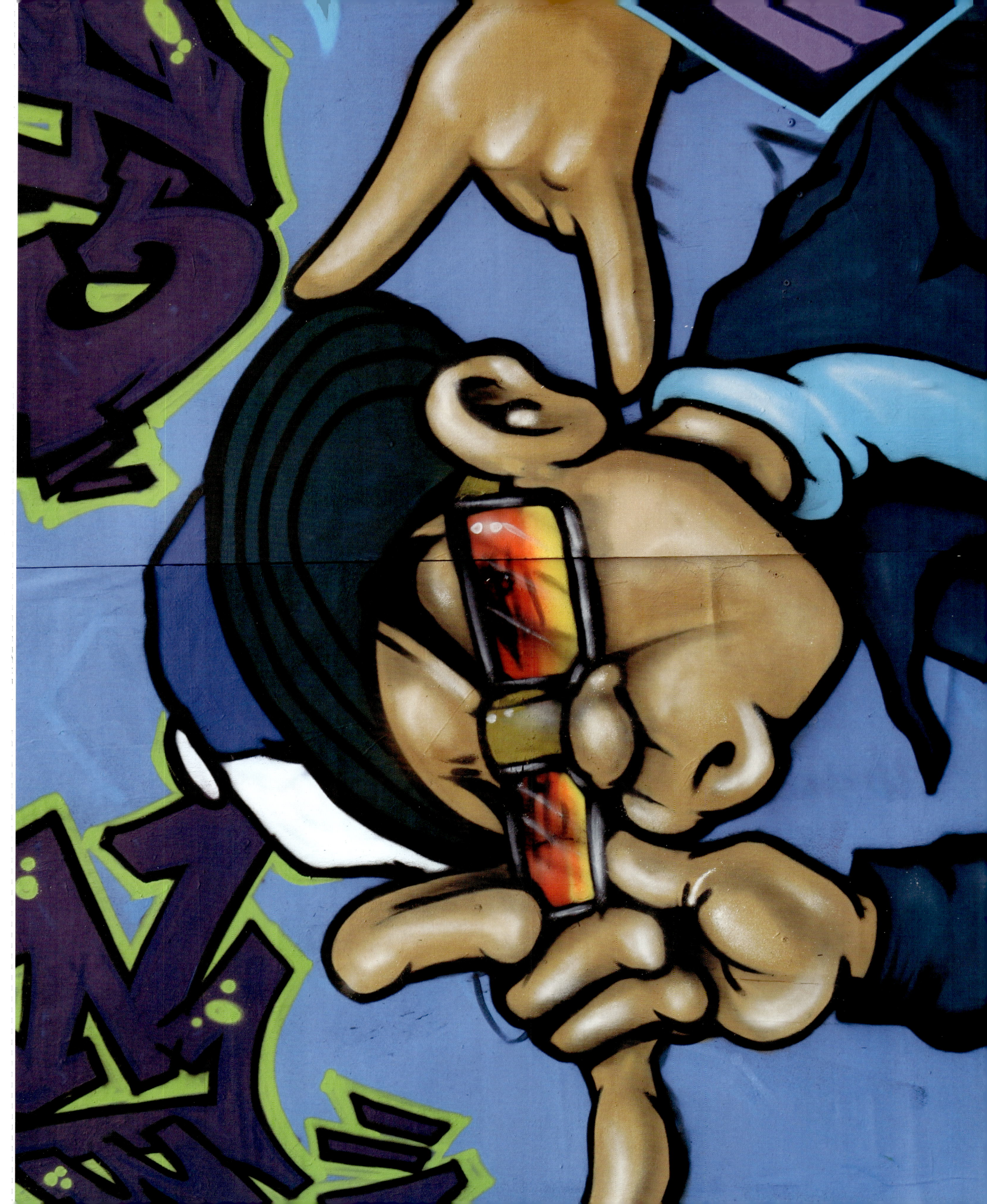

PFunk BBoy

Artist: PFunk UW DOA
Commissioned by: 3rd EyE Open
Location: Wing's Court, New Bedford, Massachusetts
Photographer: Kim Goddard

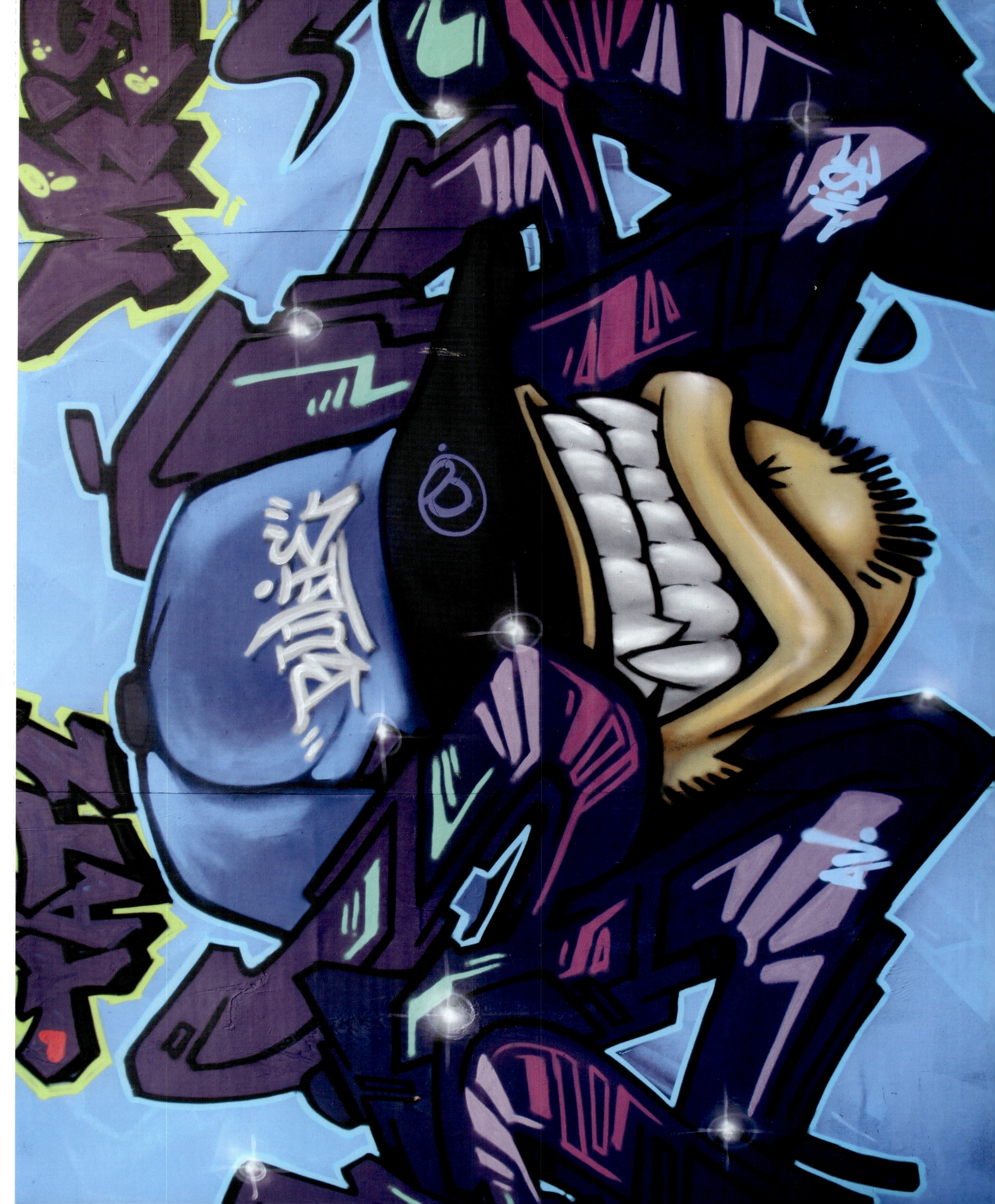

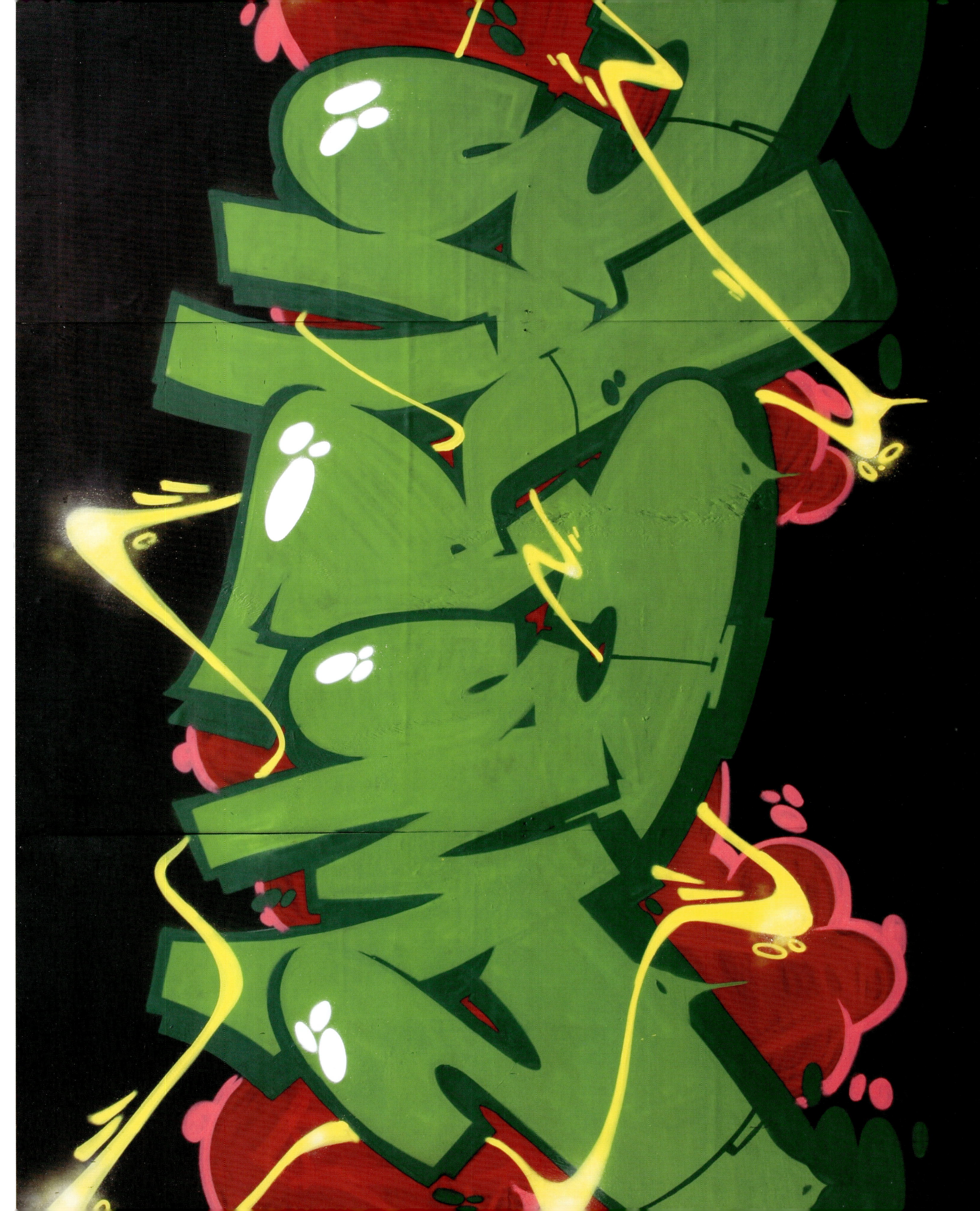

Swerve

Artist: Swerve DBM TF
Commissioned by: 3rd EyE Open
Location: Wing's Court, New Bedford, Massachusetts
Photographer: Kim Goddard

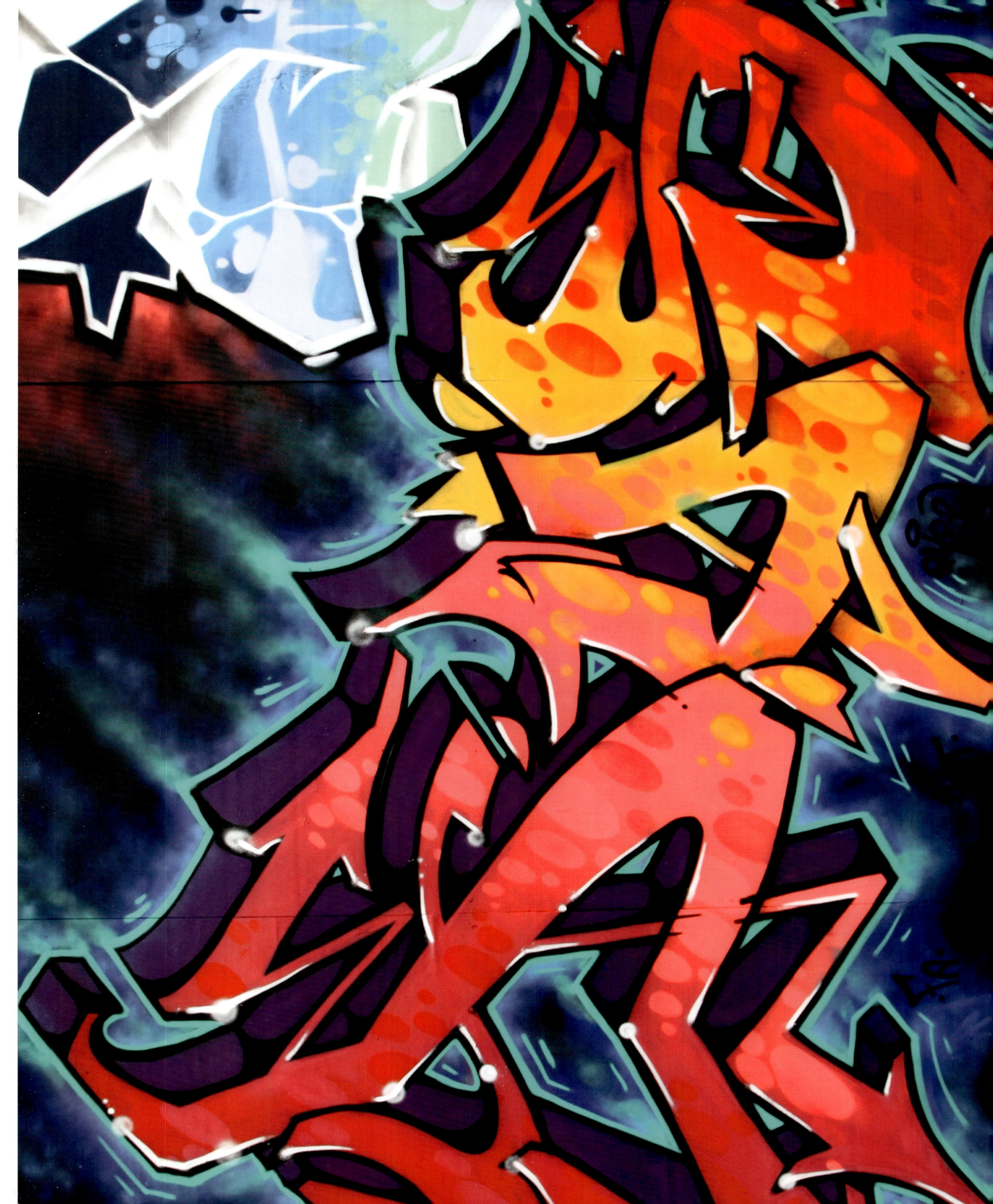

Jus1

Artist: Jus1 DBM TF
Commissioned by: 3rd EyE Open
Location: Wing's Court, New Bedford, Massachusetts
Photographer: Kim Goddard

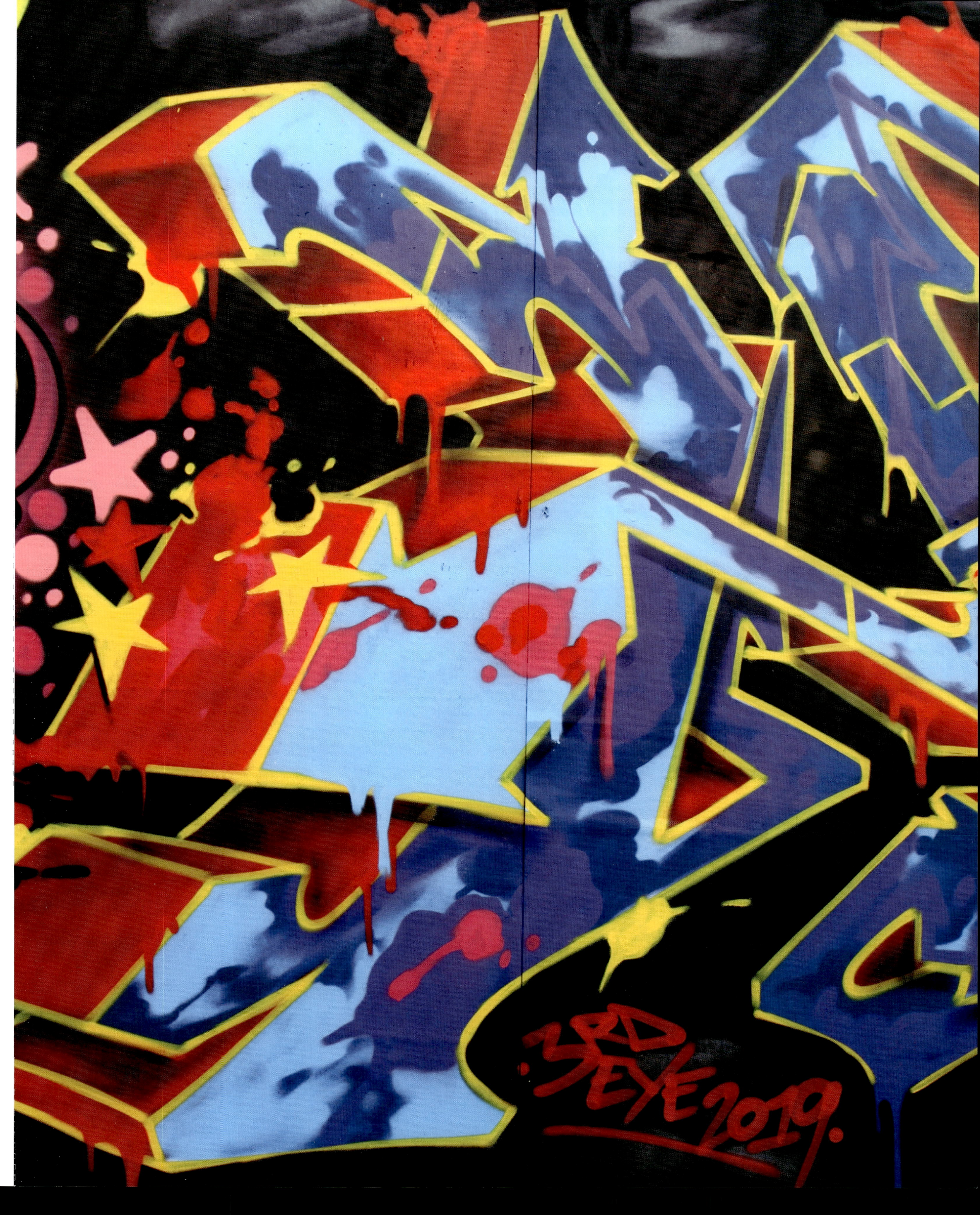
3RD
EYE 2019.

Mad1

Artist: Mad1 DBM UW
Commissioned by: 3rd EyE Open
Location: Wing's Court, New Bedford, Massachusetts
Photographer: Kim Goddard

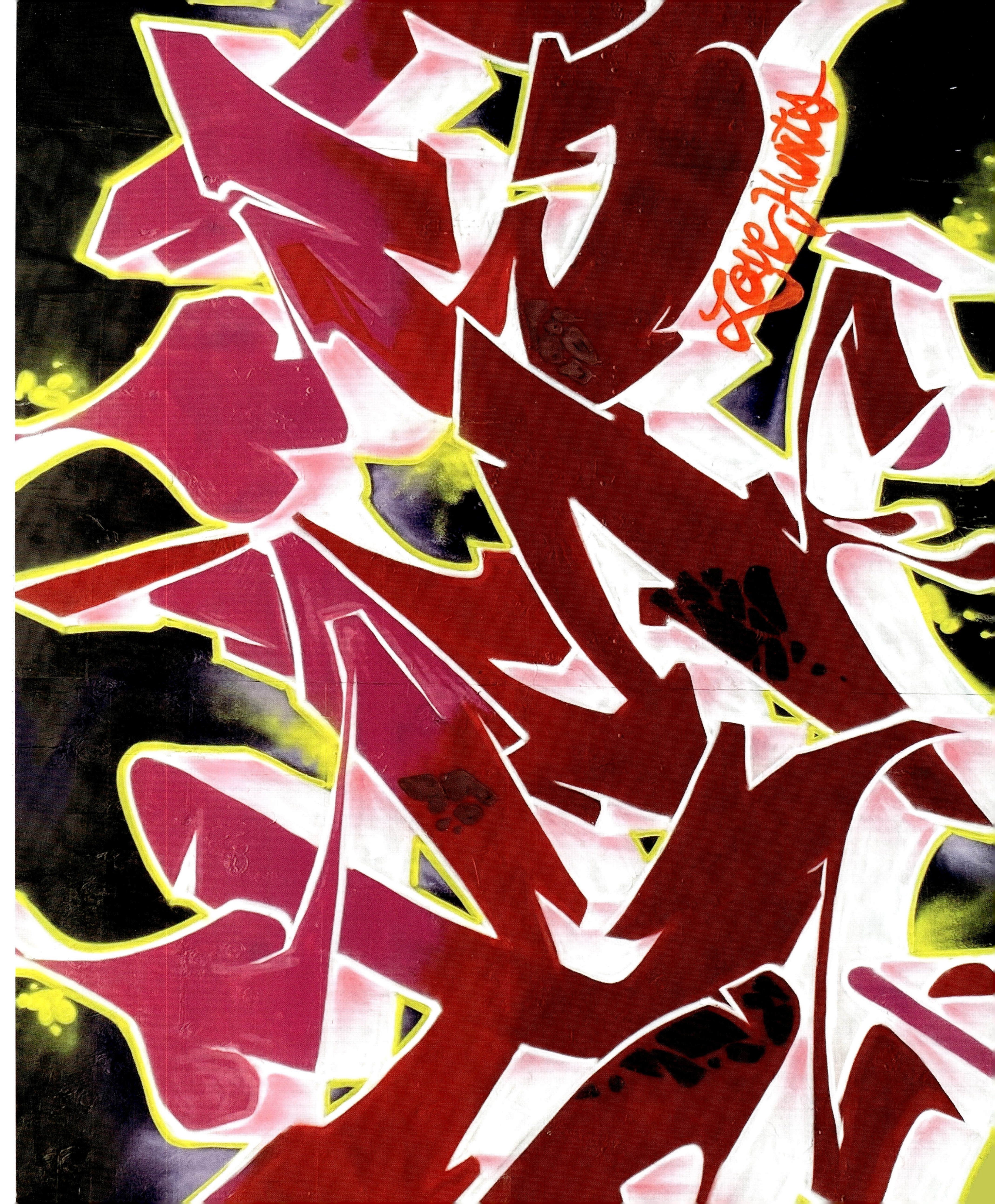
Love Hurts

ATSET

Artist: ATSET DBM TF
Commissioned by: 3rd EyE Open
Location: Wing's Court, New Bedford, Massachusetts
Photographer: Tony Nonose

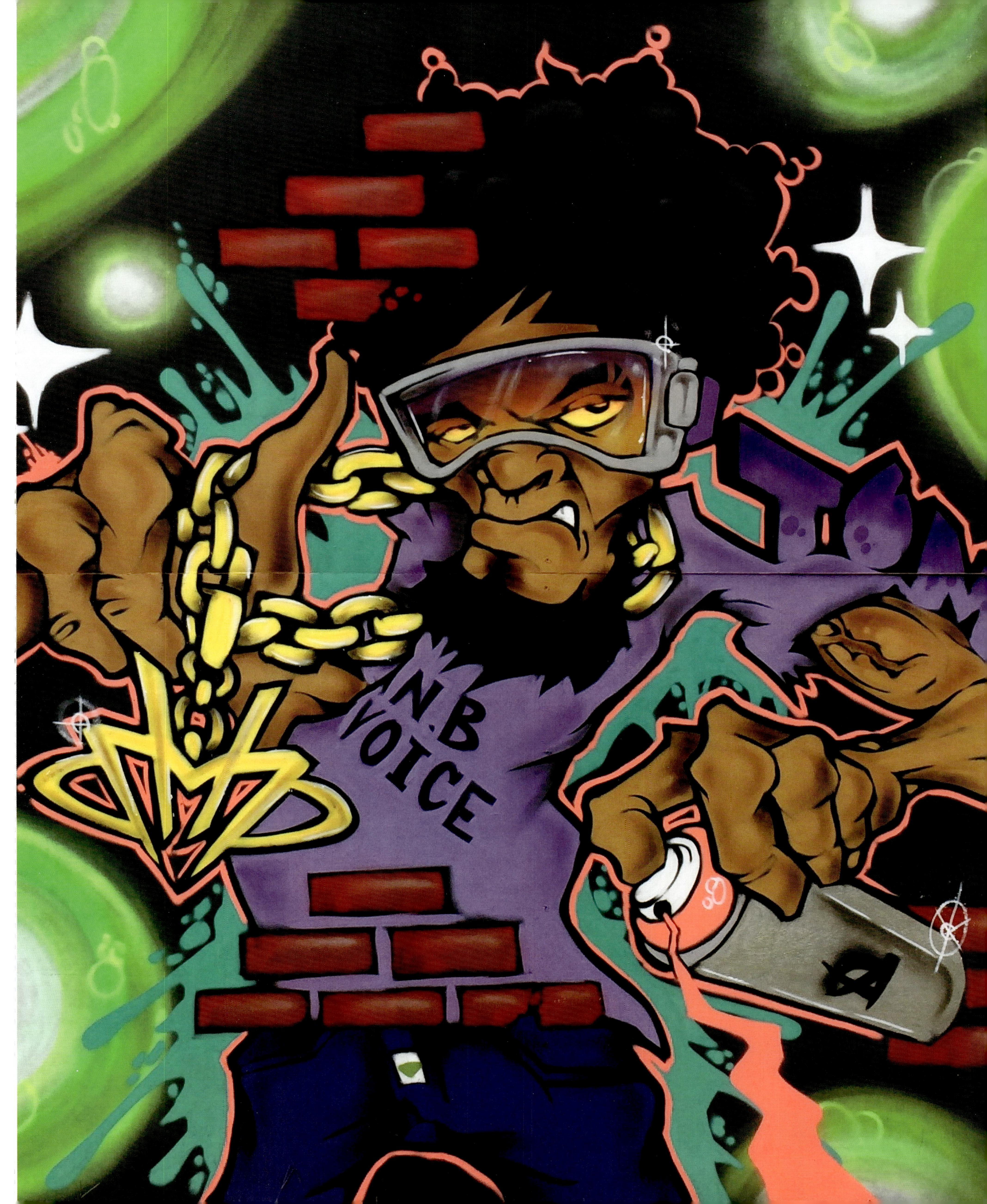
N.B
VOICE

ATSET BBOY

Artist: ATSET DBM TF
Commissioned by: 3rd EyE Open
Location: New Bedford Whaling National Historical Park, New Bedford, Massachusetts
Photographer: Kim Goddard

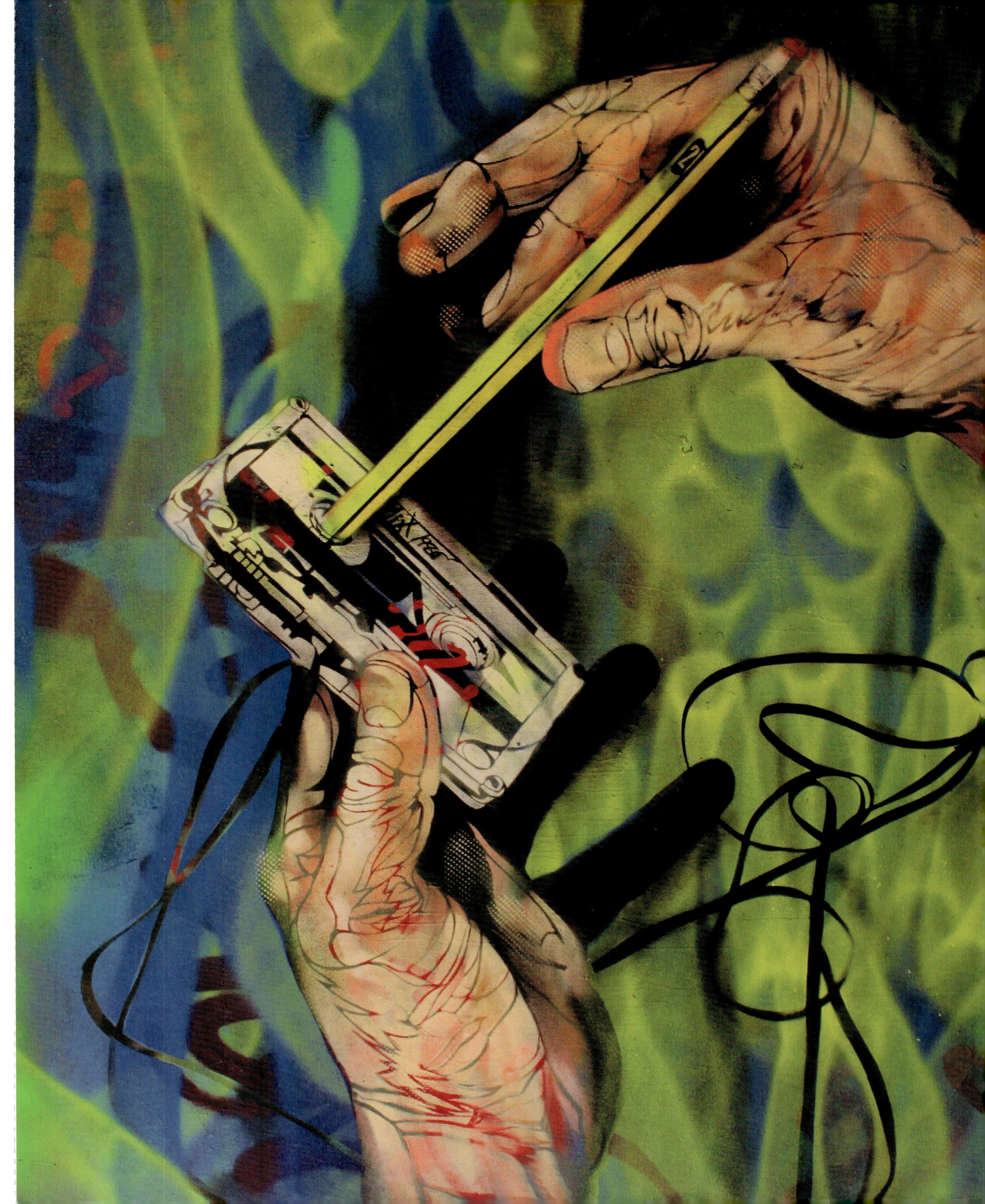

Mix Tape 86

Artist: Boston Maki
Commissioned by: Mark Carvalho
Location: Wing's Court, New Bedford, Massachusetts
Photographer: Mark Carvalho

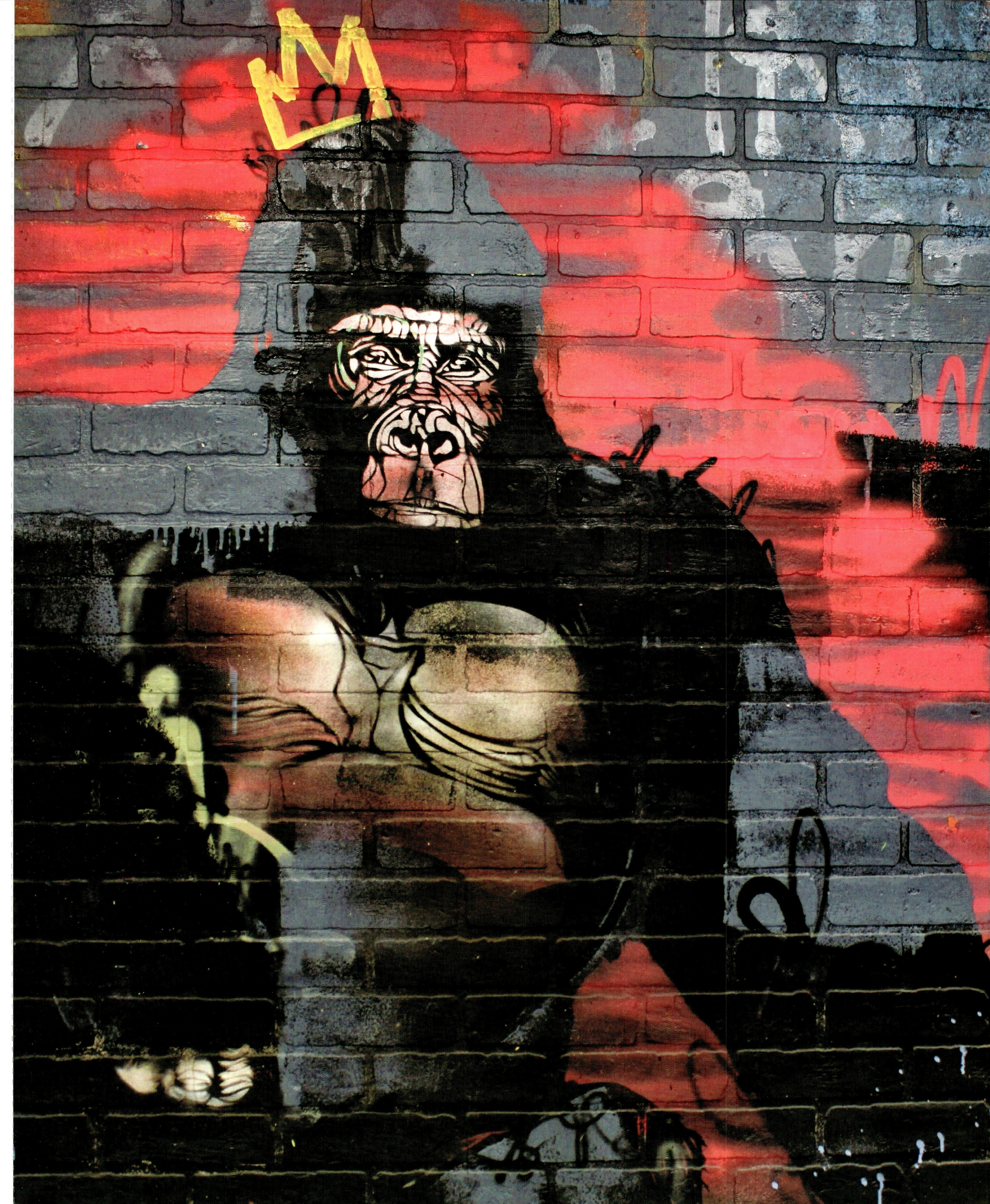

Top Banana

Artist: Boston Maki
Commissioned by: Mark Carvalho
Location: Wing's Court, New Bedford, Massachusetts
Photographer: Mark Carvalho

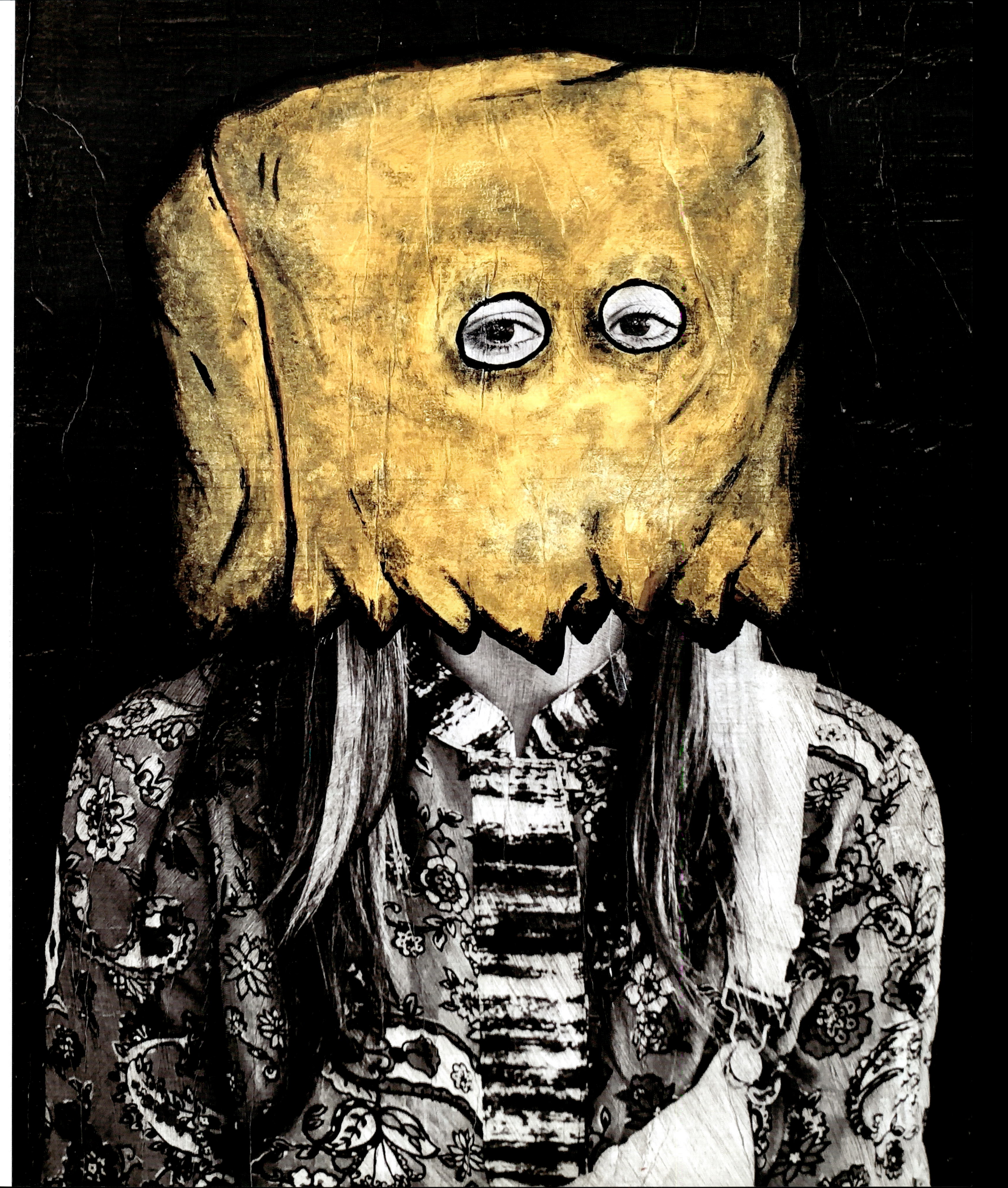

Paper Bag

Artist: Meaggsy
Commissioned by: We Art NB
Location: Acushnet Avenue, New Bedford, Massachusetts
Photographer: Meagan Borges

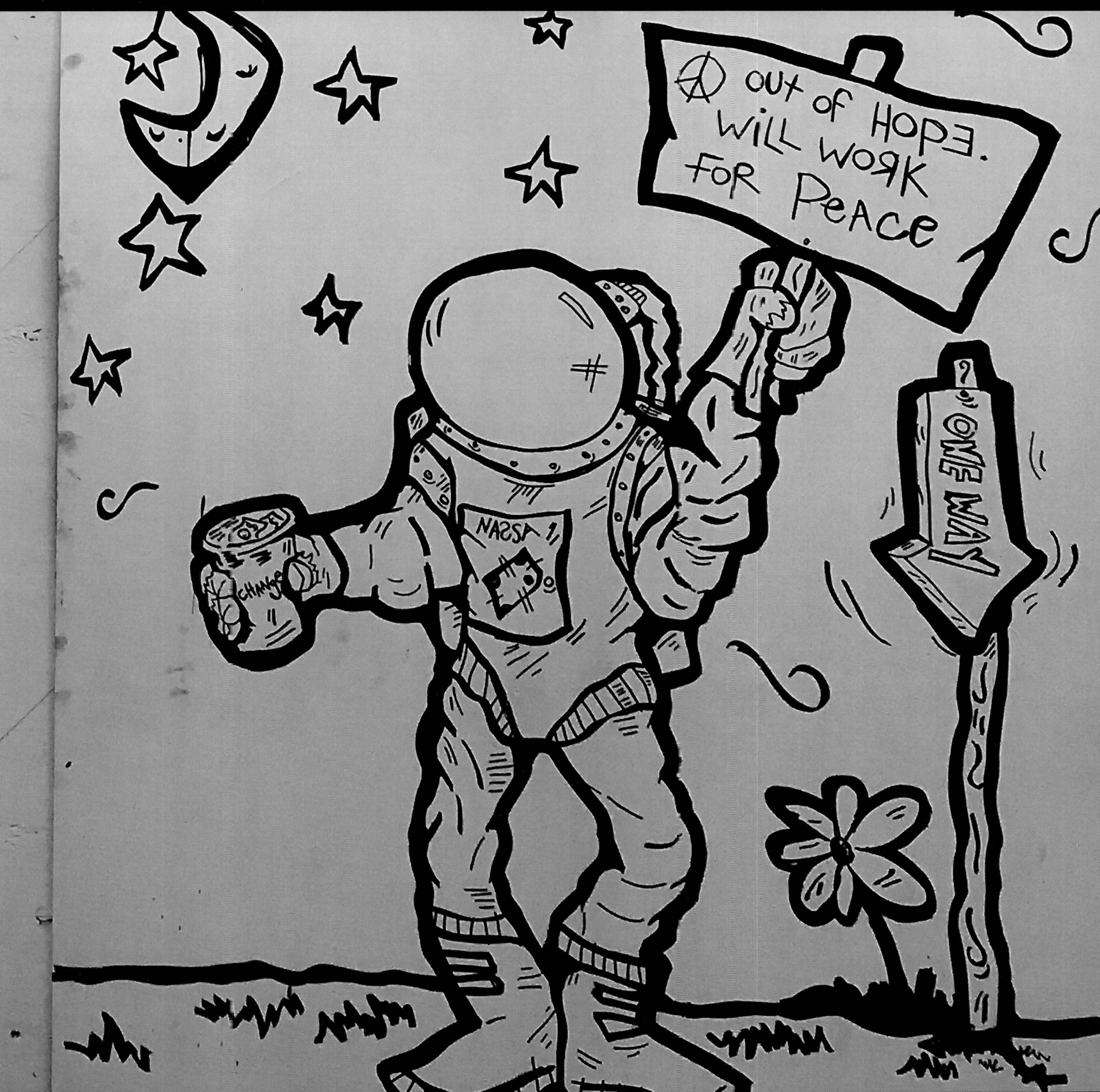

OUT OF HOPE.
WILL WORK
FOR PEACE
NASA
CHANGE
ONE WAY

Lost in Space

Artist: Meaggsy
Commissioned by: We Art NB
Location: Acushnet Avenue, New Bedford, Massachusetts
Photographer: Meagan Borges

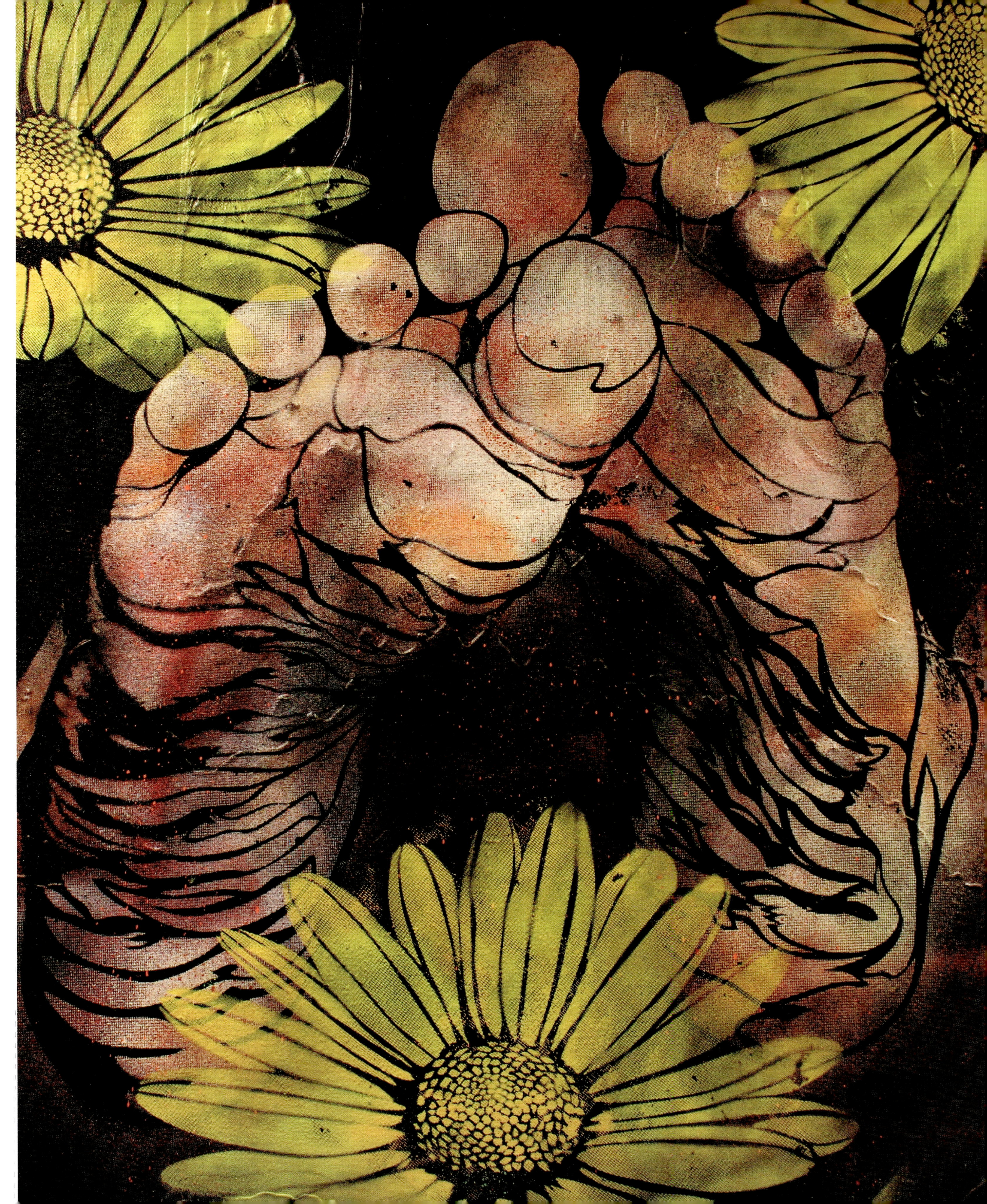

Til My Last Breath

Artist: Boston Maki
Commissioned by: Co-Creative Art Jam
Location: Wing's Court, New Bedford, Massachusetts
Photographer: Mark Carvalho

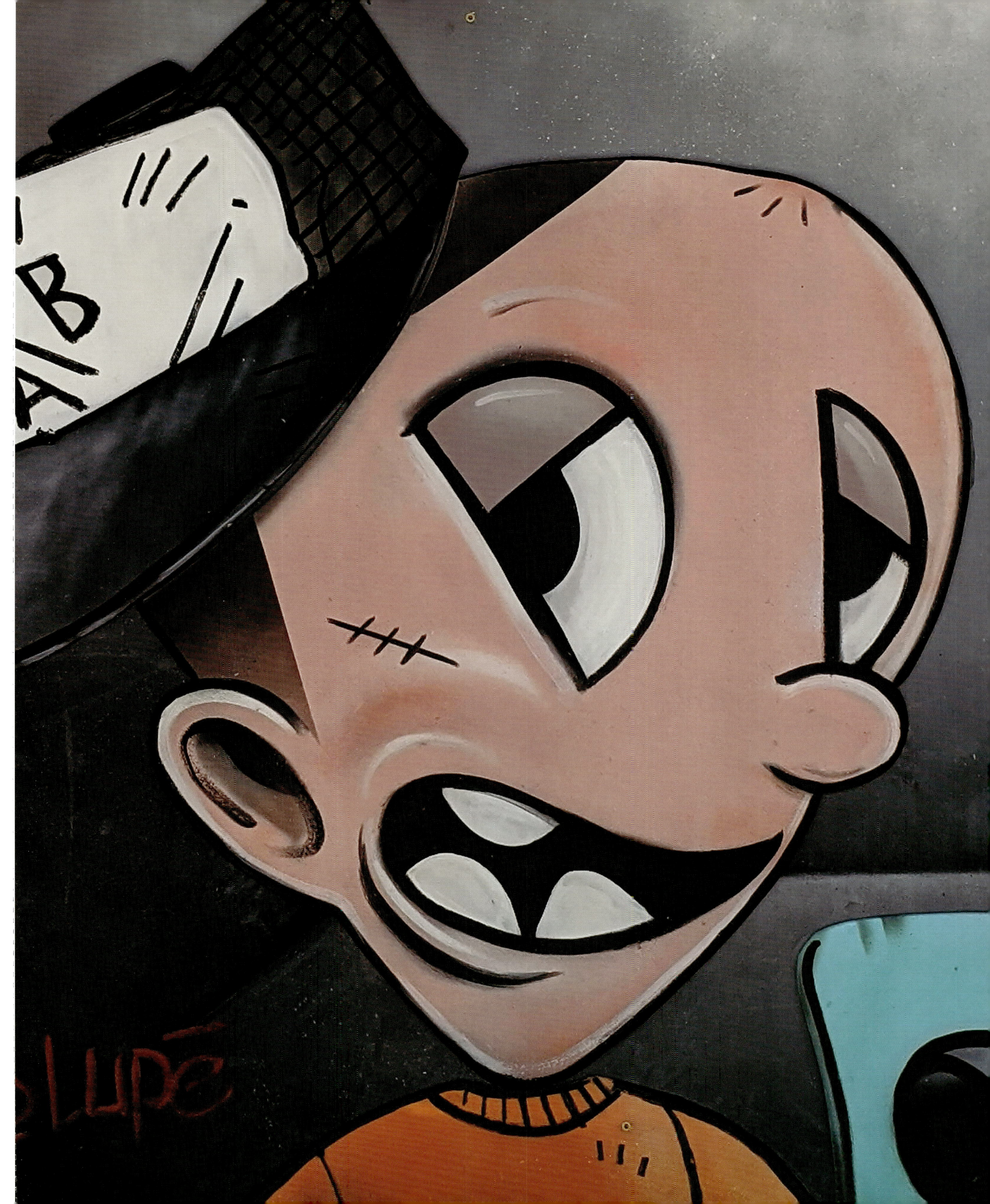
B
A
LUPE

Tholstice da Great

Artist: D Lupé
Commissioned by: No Problemo
Location: 3rd EyE Open
Photographer: Kim Goddard

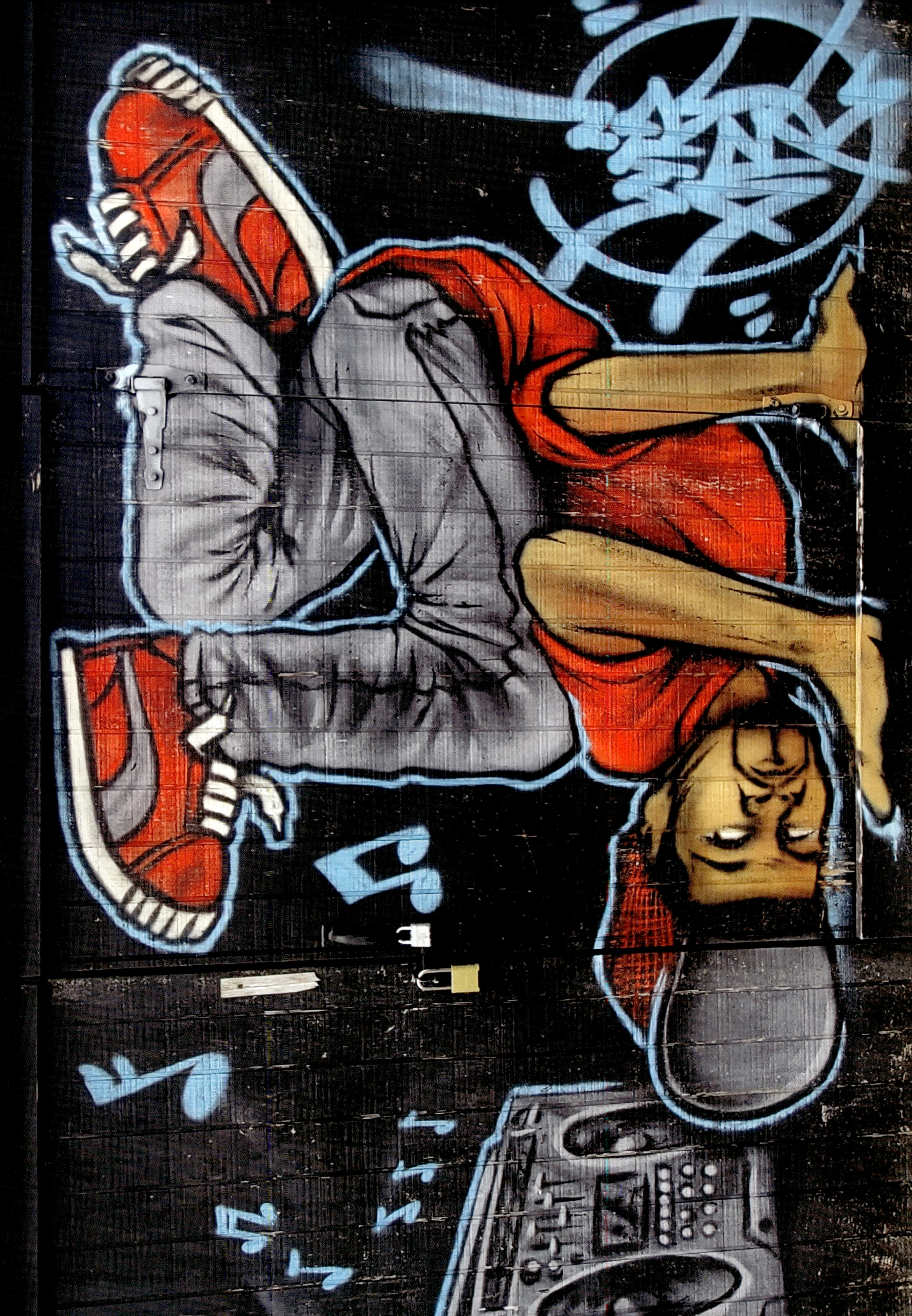

WizArt BBoy

Artist: WizArt UW DBM
Commissioned by: 3rd EyE Open
Location: Wing's Court, New Bedford, Massachusetts
Photographer: Dena Haden

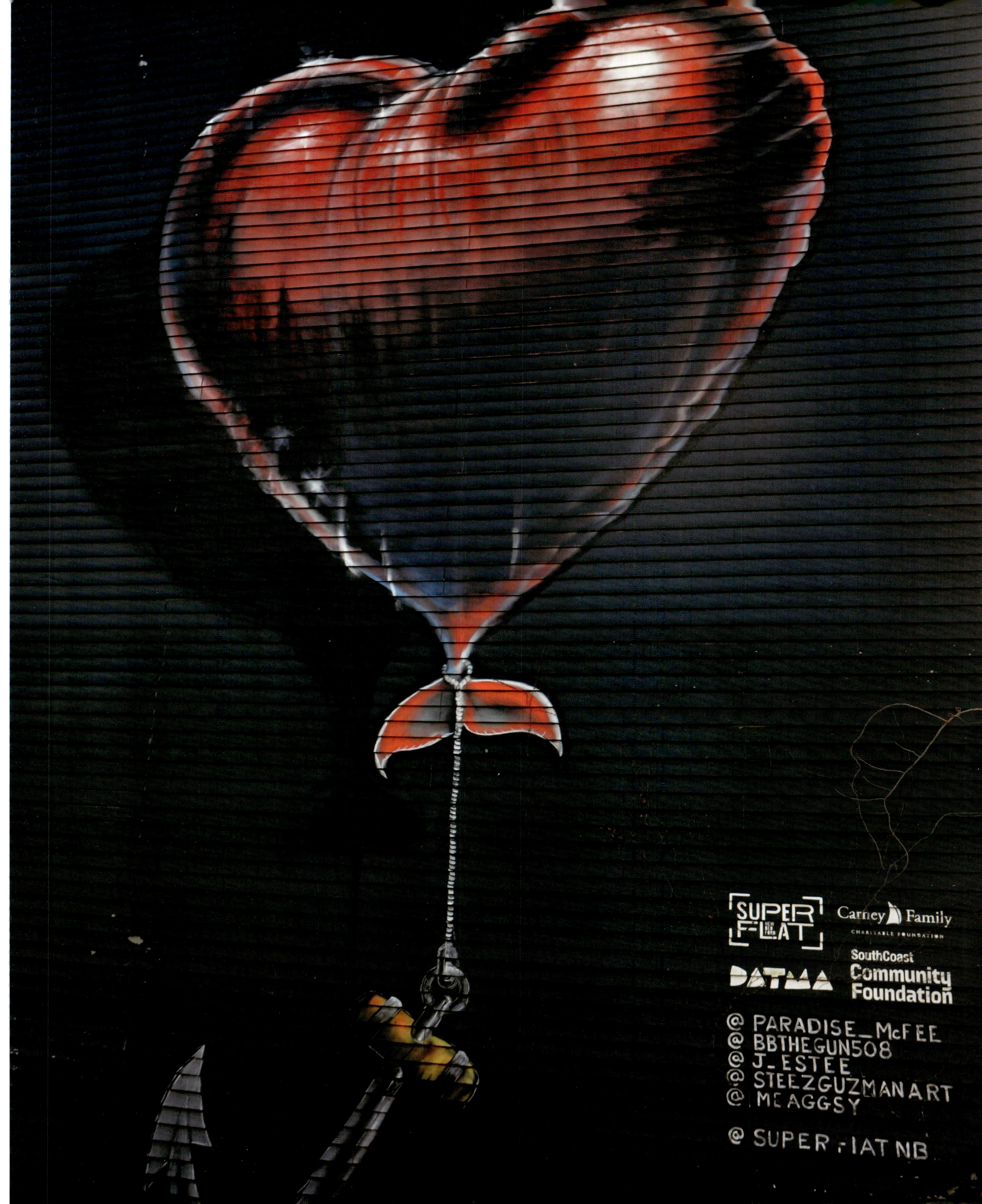

SUPER
NEW BED FORD
FLAT
Carney Family
CHARITABLE FOUNDATION
DATMA
SouthCoast
Community
Foundation
@ PARADISE_McFEE
@ BBTHEGUN508
@ J_ESTEE
@ STEEZGUZMANART
@ MEAGGSY
@ SUPERFLAT NB

Love Wins

Artist: Ryan McFee
Commissioned by: DATMA
Location: Superflat Wall, Acushnet Avenue, New Bedford, Massachusetts
Photographer: Dena Haden

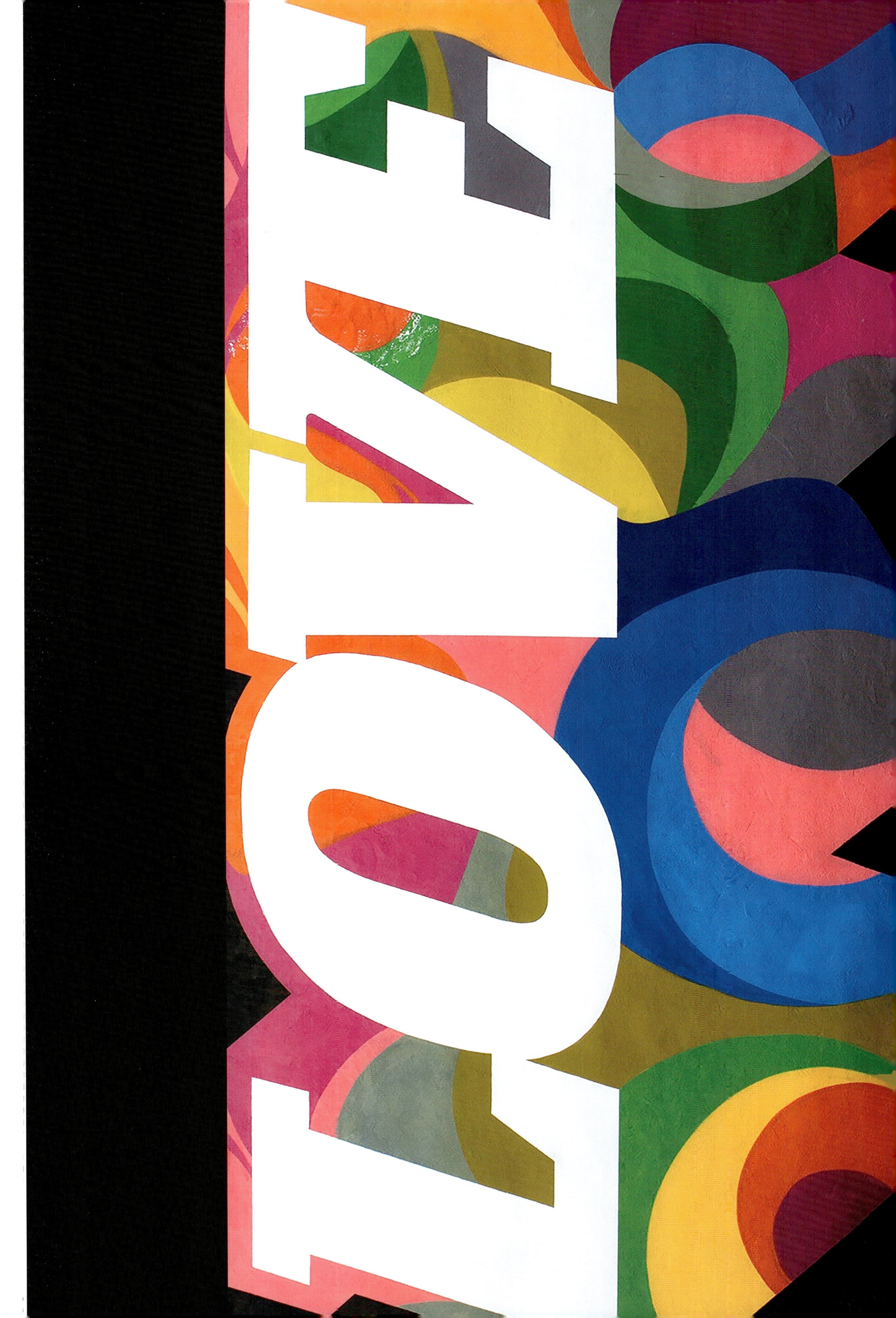

Love Rainbow

Artist: Cey Adams
Commissioned by: 3rd EyE Open
Location: Wing's Court, New Bedford, Massachusetts
Photographer: Merri Cyr

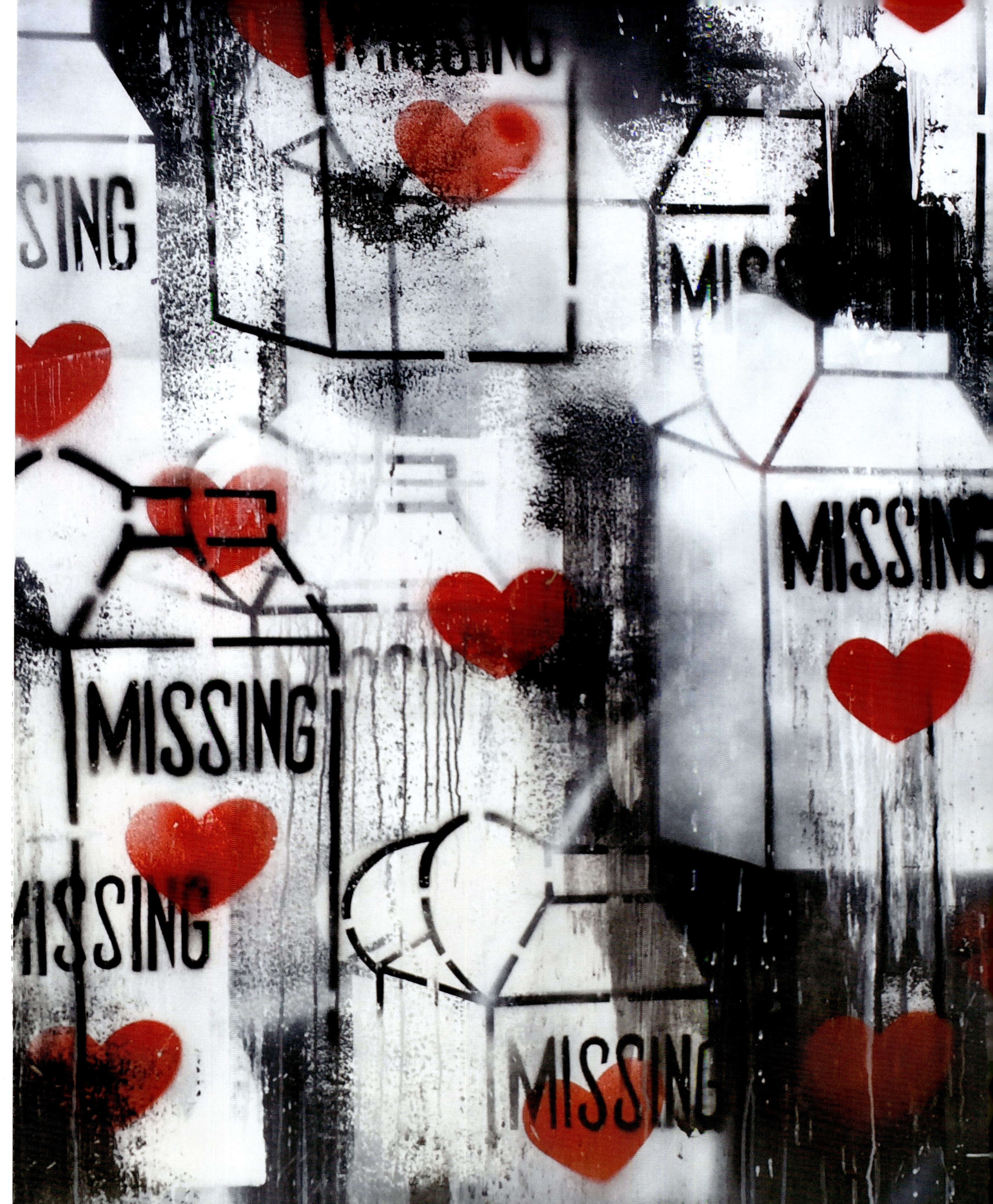

MISSING
MISSING
MISSING
MISSING
MISSING
MISSING
MISSING

Love Vandal

Artist: D Lupé
Commissioned by: Superflat Art Jam
Location: Co-Creative Center, New Bedford, Massachusetts
Photographer: Kim Goddard

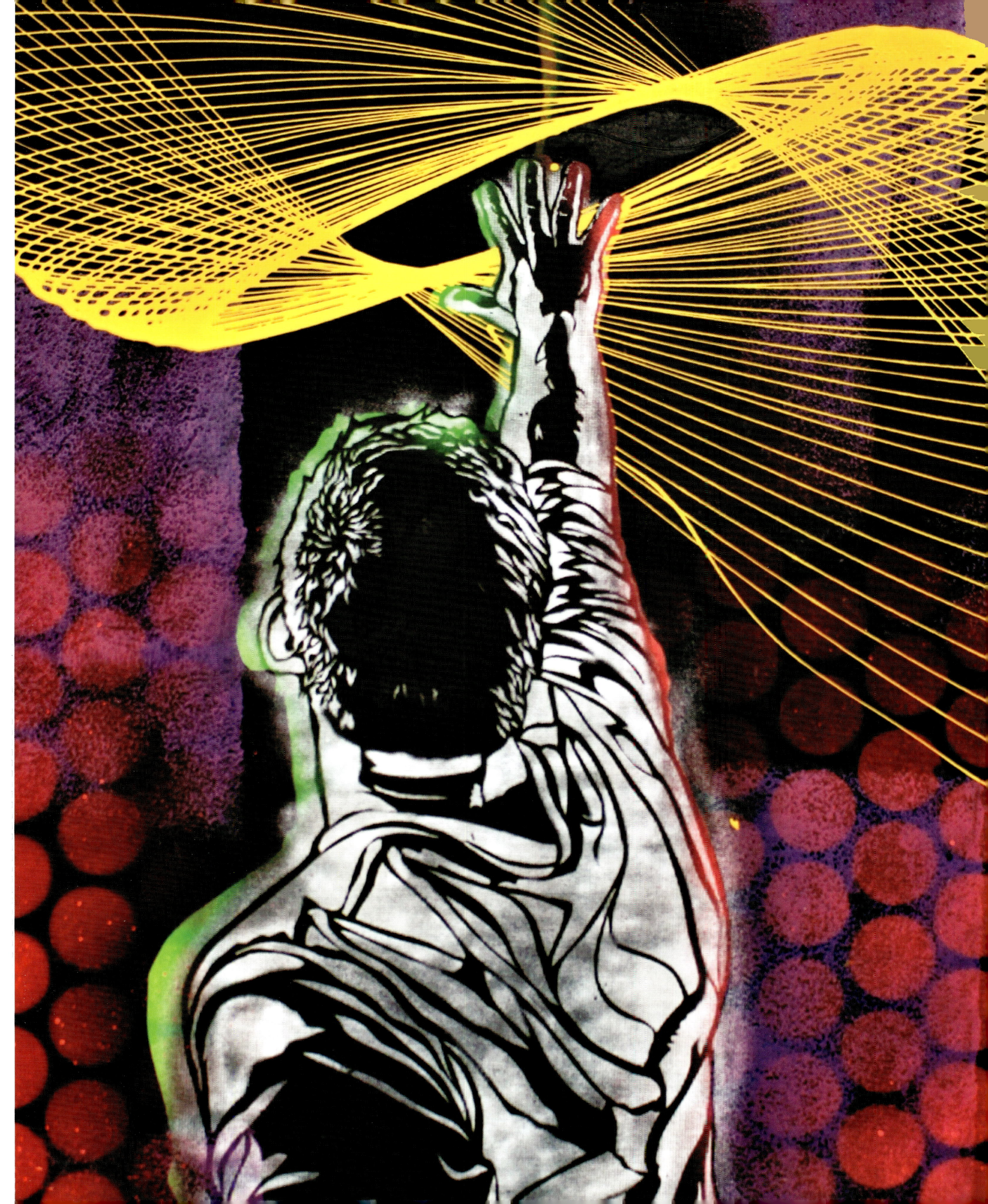

Keep Reaching

Artist: Boston Maki
Commissioned by: Meta
Location: Kilburn Mill, New Bedford, Massachusetts
Photographer: Mark Carvalho

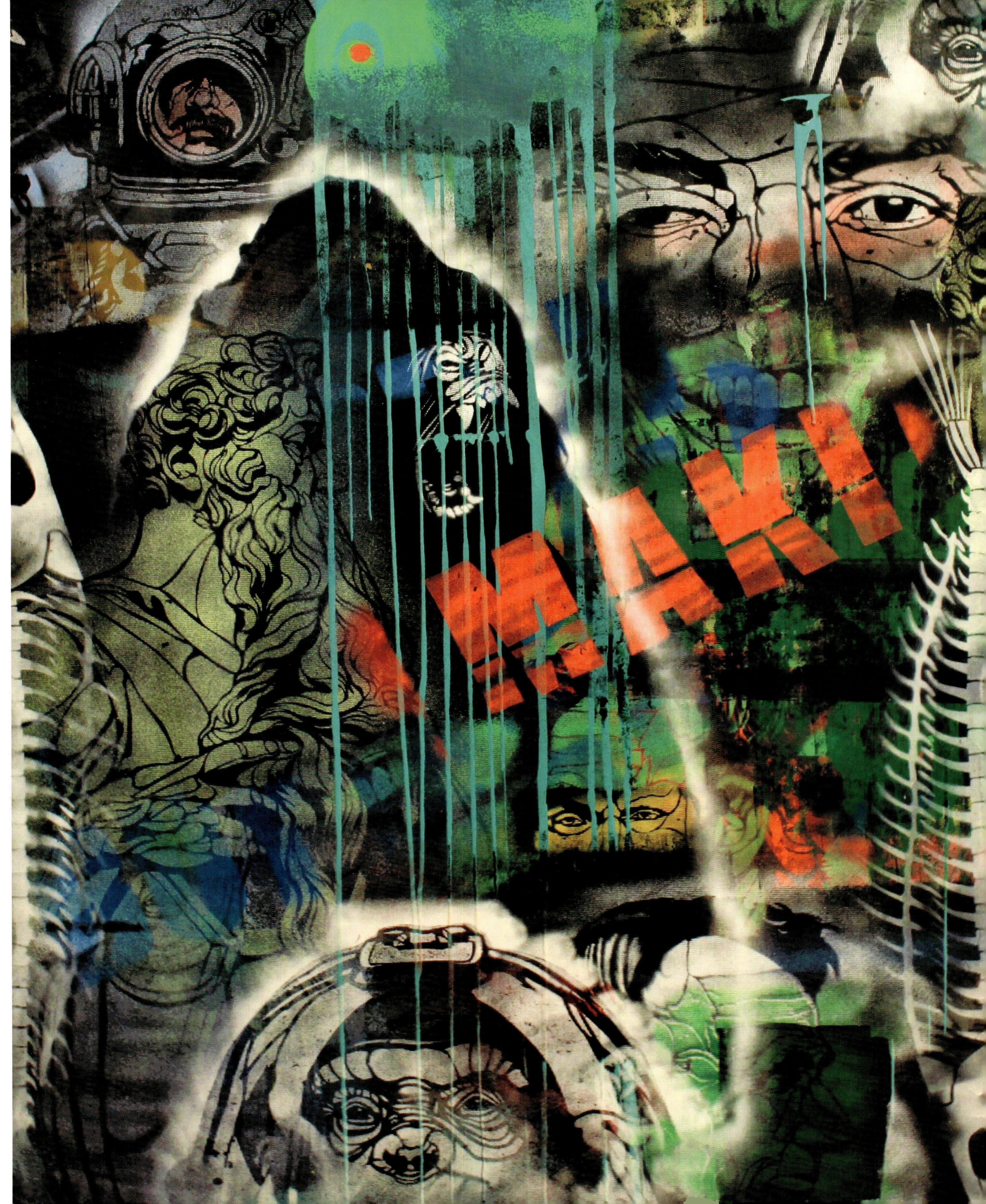

MAKI

Mashup #2017

Artist: Boston Maki
Commissioned by: Meta
Location: New England Boiler Repair, New Bedford, Massachusetts
Photographer: Mark Carvalho

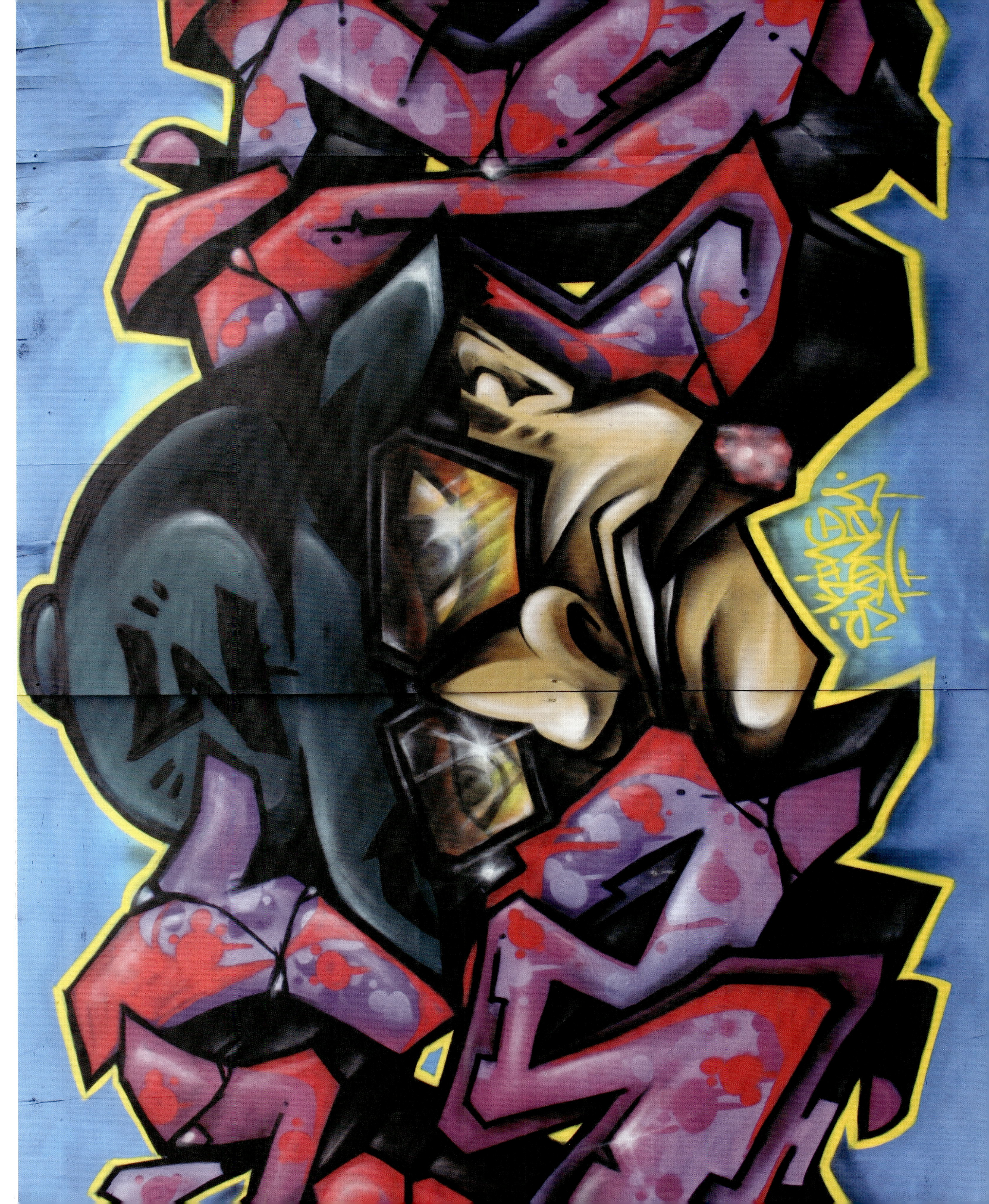

Went One BBoy

Artist: Went One DBM TF
Commissioned by: 3rd EyE Open
Location: Wing's Court, New Bedford, Massachusetts
Photographer: Kim Goddard

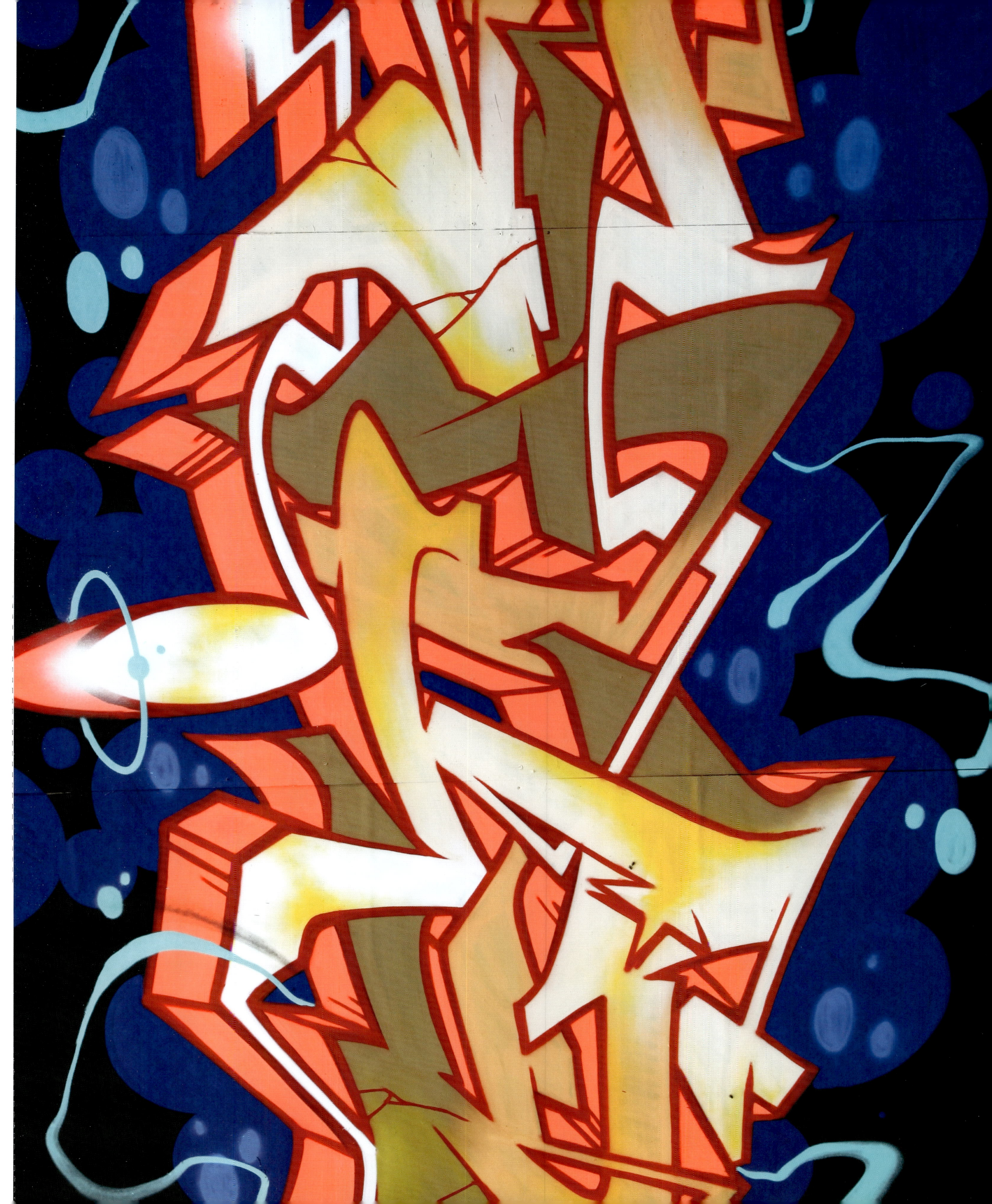

Etips

Artist: Etips DBM TF
Commissioned by: 3rd EyE Open
Location: Wing's Court, New Bedford, Massachusetts
Photographer: Kim Goddard

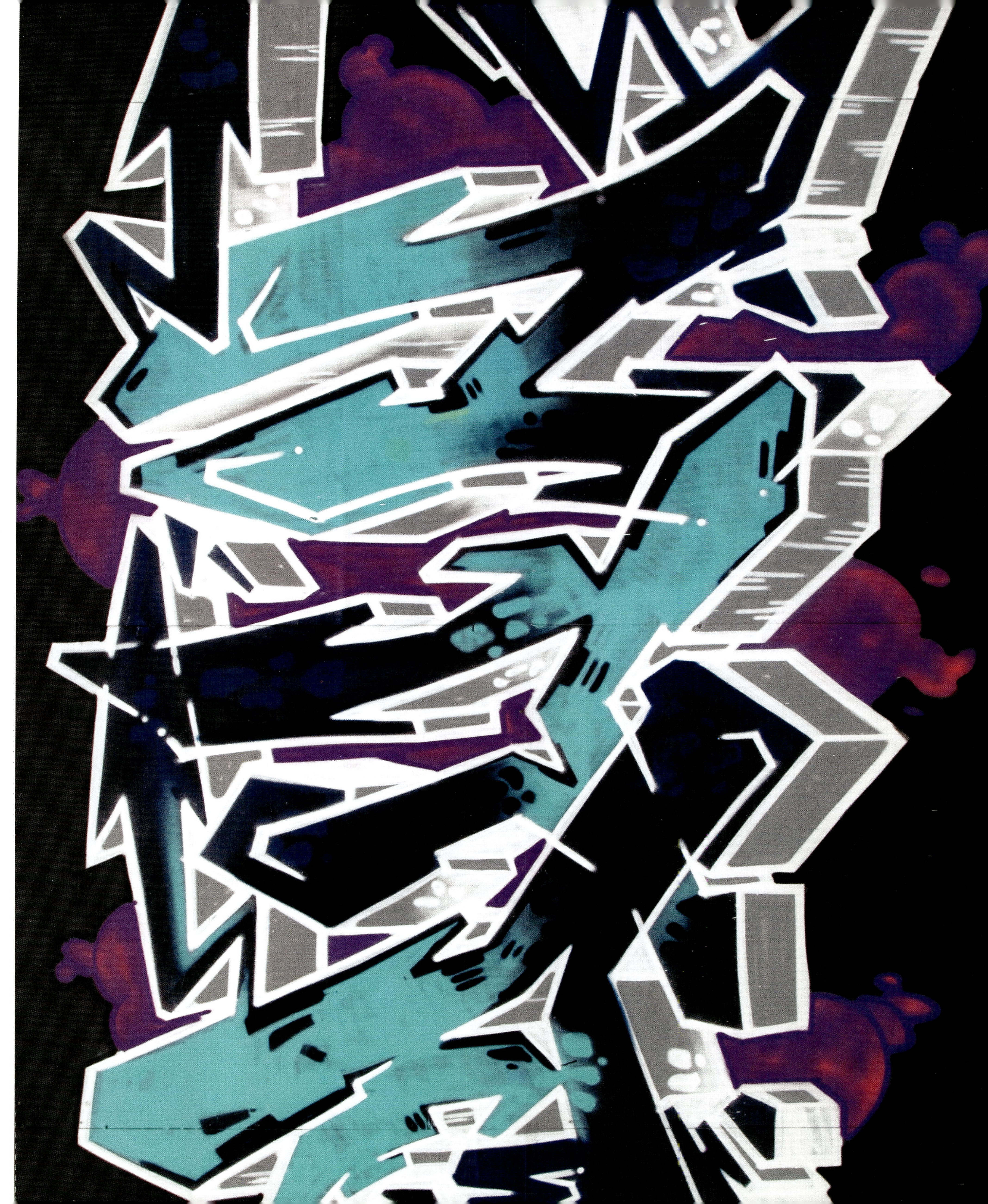

Dun1

Artist: Dun1 DBM TF
Commissioned by: 3rd EyE Open
Location: Wing's Court, New Bedford, Massachusetts
Photographer: Kim Goddard

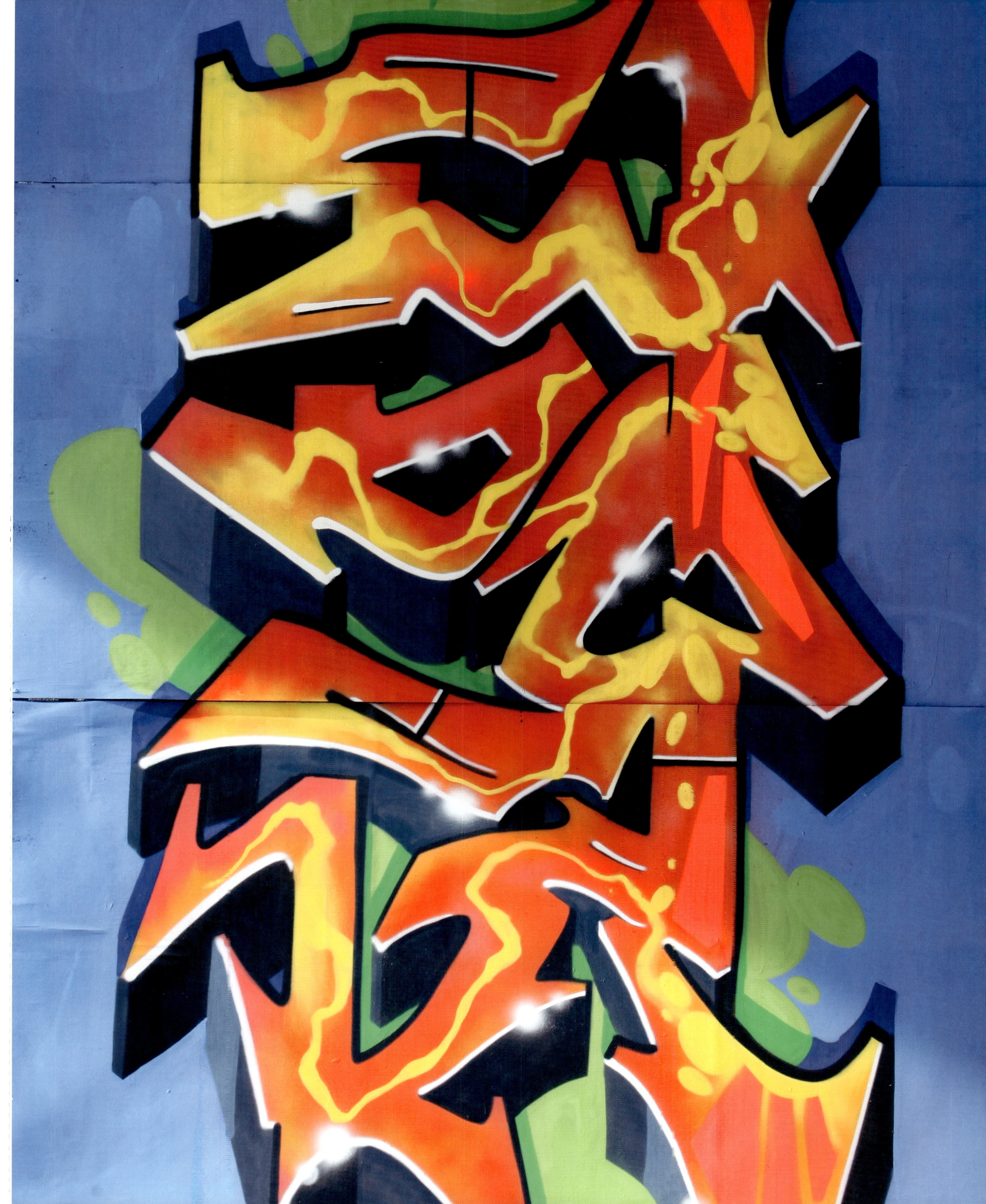

piece#1323

Artist: Sloe Outcasts MW
Commissioned by: 3rd EyE Open
Location: Wing's Court, New Bedford, Massachusetts
Photographer: Kim Goddard

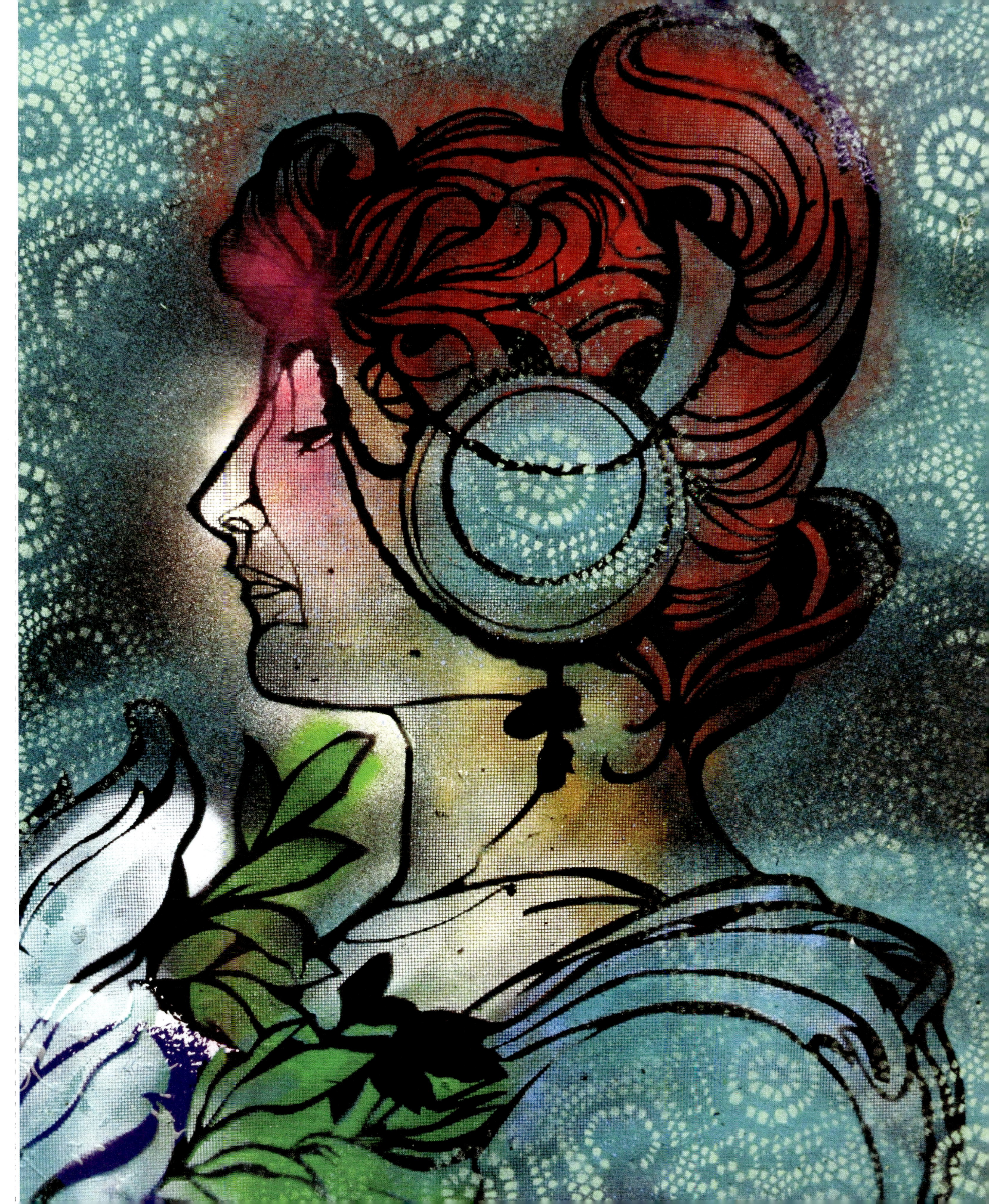

Mother Earth

Artist: Boston Maki
Commissioned by: Co-Creative Art Jam
Location: Acushnet Avenue, New Bedford, Massachusetts
Photographer: Mark Carvalho

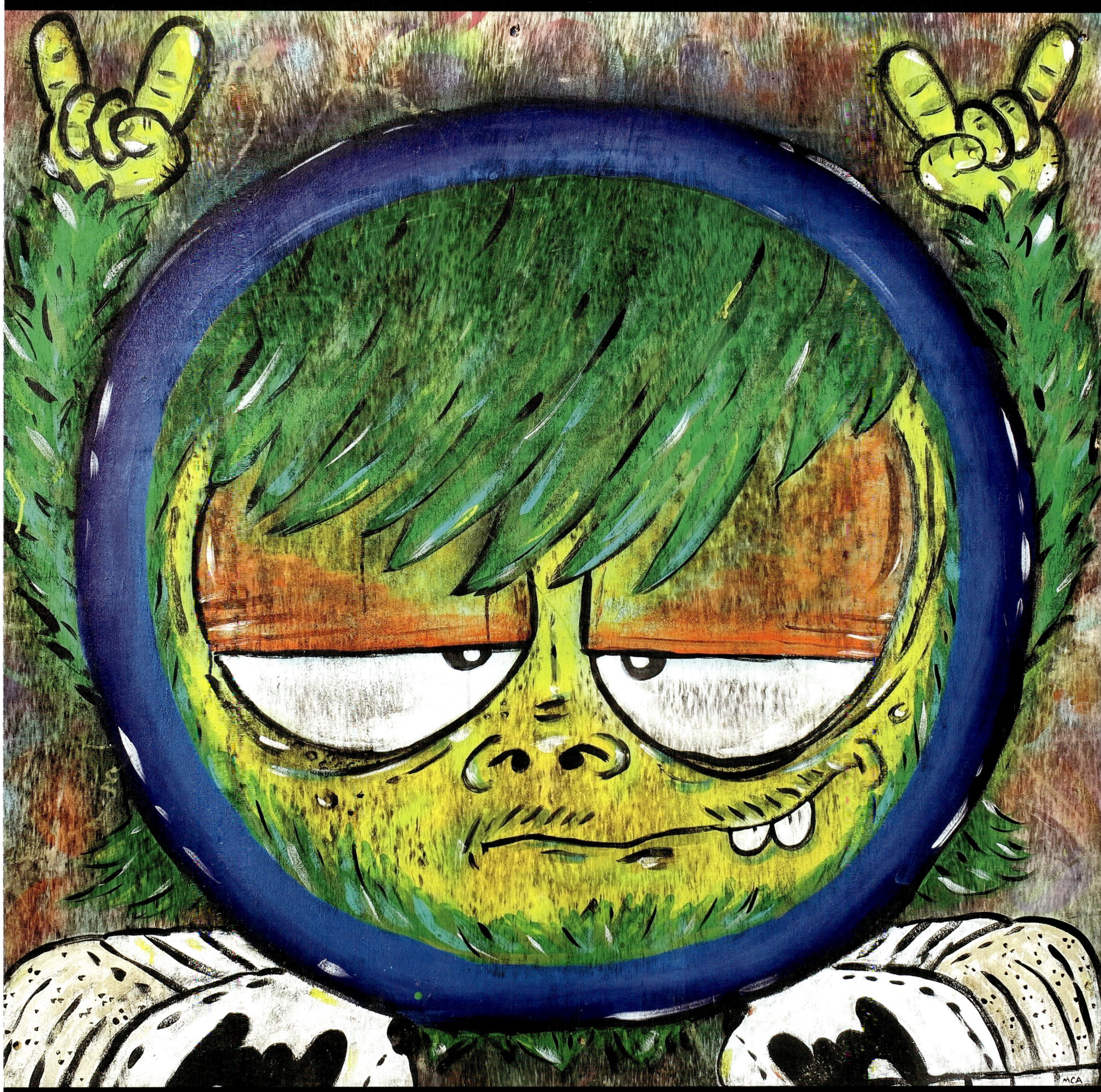

Evil O

Artist: MCA
Commissioned by: New Bedford Is Lit
Location: Acushnet Avenue, New Bedford, Massachusetts
Photographer: Jeremiah Hernandez

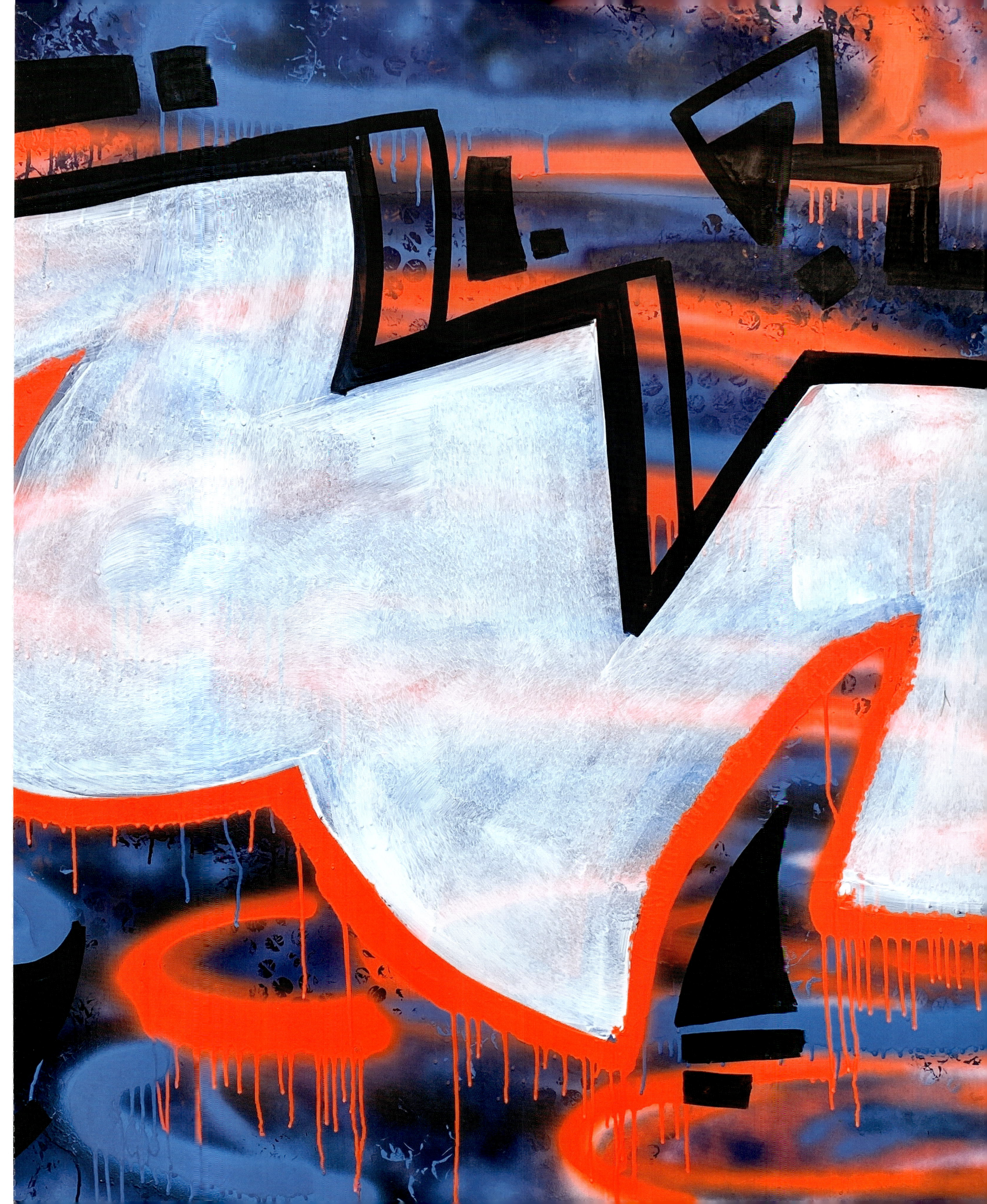

W

Artist: Jacob Ginga
Commissioned by: New Bedford Is Lit
Location: Acushnet Avenue, New Bedford, Massachusetts
Photographer: Jacob Ginga